Litvinenko Murder Case SOLVED

The Final Conclusion to this Puzzling and
Long-Unsolved Mystery

By William Dunkerley

ⓟ Omnicom Press

Published by
Omnicom Press
New Britain, CT, USA
Publishers since 1981

www.OmnicomPress.com

Library of Congress Control Number: 2015907553
ISBN-10: 0990452913
ISBN-13: 978-0-9904529-1-1
Printed in the United States of America

This book is dedicated to the pursuit of practical, fact-based solutions to troubling international conflicts and dilemmas.

Preface

--Alexander Litvinenko was a former KGB spy.

--He dictated a deathbed statement blaming Putin for poisoning him.

--The London coroner was charged with making a positive ID of the killer.

--A public inquiry was convened to give transparency to the investigation.

Each one of those sentences has something wrong with it. Can you recognize what it is?

Probably you can't. If you've relied upon the media for whatever you may know about the Litvinenko case, chances are that you can see nothing problematic in those statements. But they are all surely problematic.

There is far more to the mysterious Litvinenko death than meets the eye. There's more to it than you can glean from mass media reports.

That's because there is a surprising mystery behind the mystery. The media have addressed only the part that lies on the surface. That means if you've relied upon news reports you've gotten only half the story.

I wrote this book to fill you in on the other half. There is a dramatic behind-the-scenes story in the Litvinenko murder mystery. That's what I'll chronicle for you here.

You'll learn about the little-known mystery behind the mystery.

--Why did the case attract so much media attention?
--Was state sponsored terrorism involved?
--Who masterminded the whole thing?
--Was Litvinenko really murdered?
--What about the rogue coroner who refused to do his job?
--What went wrong with the inquest, and why did it collapse?
--How was the case politicized at the highest

levels of UK government?

This book will answer these and other questions. It will open your eyes to an entirely new dimension. By the time you finish reading the book you'll have greater insights into the Litvinenko case than almost anyone else on earth!

I begin by providing some general background to give you an overview of the case from the start.

Then I present and analyze the mysterious undercurrents that run through it all.

And in the end I present the only practical solution.

W.D.
June 2015

Contents

Chapter 1
A Mysteriously Big Story

How a little-known figure captured major headlines worldwide.

WITH urgency in his words an obviously perplexed American journalist based in Moscow reached out to me. He was in a tizzy over an avalanche of news stories that were swirling around an emergent international incident. November 19, 2006 was the date.

"I simply don't get this 'poisoning-of-Litvinenko' story," he exclaimed. He was talking about the newly-minted British citizen Alexander Litvinenko, originally from Russia. The news reports were painting a very mysterious picture. This story was making top international headlines.

I wanted to find out for myself what the buzz was all about. So I took a closer look online. A headline from the French news agency AFP seemed to sum it up: "Russian ex-spy and Putin opponent fights for his life after poisoning." All signs were pointing toward attempted murder.

This criminal act is said to have been committed back on November 1. But I didn't see it explode upon the Western news scene until almost three weeks later. I remember asking myself "why is this just breaking now?"

Was the news kept under wraps only to be released at a propitious time? Whose purpose might that serve? What was so propitious about this particular time? And why did a story about a little-known character command such unprecedented news coverage?

I'll dig into these and other even murkier issues in the case. But first a little background.

Litvinenko Who?

I realize that all readers may not have the same level of familiarity with the Litvinenko saga. So let me give you a synopsis. It is an amalgamation of information I received from insiders and the results of research I conducted myself:

Keep in mind that for a long time nobody really knew who Litvinenko was. He was kind of an obscure figure.

He grew up in the Soviet Union. In the 1990s when the USSR was no more he did FBI-type work at the new Russian Federation's security service, the FSB. He was assigned to work on organized crime cases.

I don't want to belabor this part of his story. But Litvinenko eventually found himself in trouble with the government. Some say he criminally misused his authority. That got him thrown into jail.

A time came when he was released on his own recognizance. He took that opportunity to skip out for London in October of 2000 ahead of his approaching court date.

In the UK, Litvinenko ultimately snagged a job with Boris Berezovsky. A well-known Russian billionaire-tycoon, Berezovsky himself ended up hiding out in London from criminal prosecution back in Mother Russia. They made quite a pair.

Litvinenko's job was to toss out verbal firebombs at Berezovsky's arch enemy Putin. Berezovsky was angling to see Putin overthrown in a violent revolution and replaced by a monarch. No kidding. I'm not just alleging that. He said so in his own words.

Accordingly Litvinenko accused Putin of all sorts of despicable things: pedophilia, blowing up Russian apartment buildings, killing journalists, rolling back the democratic freedoms that were left after Boris Yeltsin's tenure as president, and more.

Eventually things changed. By 2006 Berezovsky's apparent perceived need for Litvinenko seemed to wane. It sounded like Litvinenko had his hours cut back. I'm not exactly clear on what kind of activities he took up elsewhere to pick up the slack.

But the next we know, Litvinenko is in the hospital -- poisoned. That was the basis of the November 19 media blitz. The main theme seemed to be that this was just another Putin mafia-like hit on a critic.

Back to the Journalist

This brings us back to the journalist's perplexity: "I simply don't get this 'poisoning-of-Litvinenko' story."

He wanted to do his own story characterizing

Litvinenko as an unlikely target for Putin.

I advised him against doing that. "I wouldn't dig too deeply into Litvinenko himself. He's not really anybody's story," I told him.

The bigger story to me was the story itself -- why and how did it grow so big? That's what I found puzzling.

It's not as if the media were reporting any facts about Putin's involvement. The only basis they had for all their sensational reports were the unsubstantiated allegations offered by people who wanted to get rid of Putin.

Realistically how did this constitute a big story? There are people making unsubstantiated allegations all the time, and they sometimes get media play. But not like Litvinenko's.

I was reminded of the case from years ago when Hillary Clinton had been accused of being behind someone's murder. *Media Matters* reported, "Rush Limbaugh resurrected his scurrilous suggestion that Sen. Hillary Rodham Clinton (D-NY) had then-deputy White House Counsel Vincent

Foster murdered while she was first lady."
This story garnered some media attention at
the time.

Like the Litvinenko case the Clinton one had
no facts to back it up. Probably the only
reason it got any significant play is because
radio broadcaster Limbaugh pushed it.

What if instead of Limbaugh, the accuser
had been someone other than such a high-
profile person? What if he had been a
disgruntled gadfly who nobody had ever
heard of? Some kind of American analog of
Litvinenko? What serious news organization
would have given even a second thought to
such valueless nonsense?

Yet the world media went gung-ho over the
Litvinenko story. Doesn't that make you
wonder why?

This story in fact grew well beyond the
November 19 coverage that had perplexed
the journalist. That's because on November
23, Litvinenko died. This really stoked the
media fire that was already ablaze about this
case.

From the November 19 media blitz until

Litvinenko died, Berezovsky associates had been quite vociferous that Putin was behind the poisoning. And that theme was incorporated widely in the news reportage.

But right after the passing, a note from Litvinenko suddenly turned up in the hands of Berezovsky cronies. They said Litvinenko had dictated it from his deathbed. In the note Litvinenko himself clearly accused Putin of trying to silence him.

Terrorism!

Some suggest another reason this story grew to such proportions is because of the manner of Litvinenko's death as it was being characterized in the press.

Officials had ruled that the effects of radioactive polonium brought about his demise. On January 5, 2007, *60 Minutes* billed the death as a case of nuclear terrorism on the streets of London.

Many news organizations really glommed onto this nuclear connection. The *New Yorker* wrote, "Litvinenko's murder was the first known case of nuclear terrorism perpetrated against an individual."

That sounds pretty scary. If you're like me you'll probably agree that this seems like a very serious matter.

Think back of the fear that had spread across post-9/11 America when anthrax letters were circulating in the mails. Were we now about to see the far deadlier polonium being used to terrorize the world?

State Sponsored Terrorism?

The persistent accusation in the press was that Litvinenko's murder was ordered by Russian president Vladimir Putin himself. This angle sure ratcheted up the level of concern.

Here we have the strong-man leader of the world's largest country. He's seriously suspected of practicing the most deadly form of terrorism imaginable, going nuclear.

What could be more frightening to so many people?

Russia is presently the only country with the nuclear capability for wiping the United States off the map. If Putin is willing to deploy nuclear material to get rid of a minor annoyance like Litvinenko, what might he do if he had a more significant international score to settle?

No wonder public interest in Litvinenko shot up so dramatically at the end of 2006. This nuclear terrorism incident could presage a lot of horrific trouble ahead for the rest of us.

Chapter 2
An Eye Opening Experience

The puzzling rise and fall of Litvinenko's fame.

AFTER that exchange with the journalist in 2006, I casually followed the Litvinenko story in the media. The nagging feeling that something was not kosher about the extent of the media coverage was a concern I just couldn't shake, though.

Jump forward in time with me for a moment: As I write this book in 2015, I decided to go back and reexamine the level of media attention that was given to the Litvinenko story in 2006 and 2007.

I turned to Google Trends for a perspective. It shows the relative amount of search interest in whatever terms you enter. In a way it's an indirect measure of fame and curiosity that may have been inspired by media reports.

The Google results are displayed along a timeline. I entered the term "Litvinenko." I also put in Putin's name as a point of comparison. I used a broad search covering the period from January 2004 to January

2009.

Aha!

What I found turned out to be quite enlightening. In the time before Litvinenko's death, interest in Putin was averaging around 6 on the Google scale.

During this same time period the relative interest in Litvinenko ranked a dead zero. There was no measurable interest in him.

This all changed when the media blitz occurred.

Now Litvinenko's name was pulling scores of 11 and 12 in November and December 2006.

Why, Litvinenko had a bigger name than even Putin. Twice as big!

How Many Minutes of Fame?

How long do you think Litvinenko's fame lasted? By February his Google Trends score had fallen down to just 2, and thereafter it has only bounced back and forth between 1 and 0. Meanwhile Putin's score has climbed upwards.

What could account for the puzzlingly dramatic rise and precipitous fall in curiosity about Litvinenko? And what really precipitated the media blitz in the first place?

Chapter 3
Back to the Past

A thorough study of the media coverage.

OKAY, so now let's go back to 2007, right after Litvinenko's death. My casual following of the case was suddenly ratcheted up to a major focus for me. You see, it was then that I was contacted by the International Federation of Journalists. The organization was preparing for its bi-annual Congress. The gathering would attract leading journalists from all over the globe.

The organizers of the Congress sought to commission me to investigate the media coverage of the Litvinenko story, and for me to make a presentation of my findings at the International Congress to be held in May 2007. I accepted the assignment and conducted very extensive research.

My Findings?

I found that the news reports on the case were fairly unanimous. A composite newspaper headline from the time might read "Ex-KGB Spy Murdered on Orders of Putin." And that's what most people who've paid any attention to the Litvinenko case have likely come to believe.

But I found there is something surprisingly wrong with this story.

You see, nothing in that headline is actually known to be true.

That's right. There is nothing there that has been connected to any reliable facts. The headline simply reflects allegations that have not been substantiated by facts. And those allegations were made by people who admittedly are dedicated to destabilizing the Russian state and replacing Putin. Their utterances seem to be the only basis of the phony narrative that became the mainstream news story.

I realize that such a massive fraud may be hard to fathom. That is testament to its effectiveness. It has been so successful that the actual facts of the case sound counterintuitive to most people.

Fabricate, Fabricate, Fabricate

Here are a few examples of falsehoods contained within the mainstream story:

--Litvinenko probably was never in his life a KGB spy. That claim was an outright fabrication. I've received clear statements from insiders with direct connections. The KGB spy moniker was likely used just to make the story sound more sensational. It seems to have no basis in fact. If you think there is such a basis, look for substantiation and tell me about it, and I'll revise my statement.

--There's no evidence to even suggest that Litvinenko's death was ever ordered by Putin. All there've been are allegations originating from arch enemies of Putin's.

Their motive for lying is clear. They want to push Putin out of the catbird's seat in Moscow and claim it for themselves or their surrogates.

Now, this does not mean I have evidence that Putin had nothing to do with Litvinenko's death. I don't. I don't know who was responsible. But neither do the journalists and politicians who have sought to incriminate Putin.

Reasons for suspecting culpability, however, seem to depend upon belief of the various other fabricated stories about Putin.

--No coroner in London has ever ruled that Litvinenko's death was an actual homicide. Litvinenko could accidentally have been contaminated by polonium. He could have committed suicide with it. All these possibilities have been alleged at various times by various people. If it really was a homicide, why didn't the coroner declare it so?

--And the final kicker? The famously reported deathbed statement that was dictated by Litvinenko accusing Putin? It was a hoax. That's a proven fact. Those words weren't Litvinenko's. Indeed, the hoaxer has even confessed, explaining that he wrote the statement himself. What's more he's admitted that he had no factual basis for the allegations he made. Yet to this day the media persists in referring to Litvinenko's deathbed statement. What do you make of that?

Do You Believe in Facts?

My claims may sound quite outlandish if you've been thinking all along that the widespread media reports were factual. But I documented my research and conclusions in the report I gave at the International Federation of Journalists' Congress. It was scrutinized by a panel of Western and Russian media experts without negating my primary findings at all.

In my report there is a lot more that is said on false news stories. In 2011, on the fifth anniversary of Litvinenko's death, I updated and expanded upon that report in my book titled *The Phony Litvinenko Murder*.

Among other things it shows that Litvinenko actually believed that someone other than Putin was responsible for his poisoning. I even reveal the mechanism through which the phony murder story went mainstream.

And I name names for who was behind the phony story.

If this aspect of the case interests you, or if you want to see proof of my above statements, I highly commend *The Phony Litvinenko Murder* for your edification.

Case Closed?

So now what do you think? Is this case

closed yet? Is the expose of the falsehoods that masqueraded as facts enough to negate all the fabrications and lies? Are you satisfied that the Litvinenko case was just an orchestrated farce?

Apparently the unvarnished truth wasn't enough for the British government. It kept up the pretense of the fabrications.

I'll detail that and explain how I helped to thwart this charade in the next chapters.

Chapter 4
The Inquest

A rogue coroner flouts British law.

I'VE got to tell you, by the time I finished writing *The Phony Litvinenko Murder* in 2011, I knew I had this case knocked. I had burst the bubble of the fabricated stories.

Little did I know that a brand new phase of the case was about to begin.

What am I talking about?

It was the big push undertaken by the British government to cover up the fabrications and validate the phony stories.

That's where this chapter picks up.

All the media reports were pointing to Putin's culpability. But my own research was telling me that the media reports were not supported by evidence.

A Break in the Case

A rude awakening came to me in the research process. It occurred when I went

looking for Litvinenko's death certificate.
That document would tell me the manner
and cause of death.

The manner of death could refer to
something like: natural causes, accidental
death, homicide, suicide, or undetermined
(if there were no clear indications of the
other manners of death). The cause of death
tells what specifically killed the person.
Examples include cardiac arrest, drowning,
overdose, automobile collision, etc.

But there was no death certificate. The
coroner's office assured me of that. This
meant that the coroner, the official charged
with ruling on the death, had not ruled. It
was then five years after the death. But it
never had been ruled a homicide.

The Murder That Wasn't

I thought that was big news. All the
mainstream media had for years been
reporting on a murder that had never been
officially declared a murder.

And that was the backdrop for the 2011
opening of the official coroner's inquest into
Litvinenko's death. I was hoping that the

coroner would now finally clear up the
mystery and rule on the manner and cause of
death.

Quickly, though, the inquest focused not on
whether or not Litvinenko was murdered.
Instead it was squarely aimed at searching
for Russian culpability. In other words, who
did it?

Isn't this ironic? Despite the coroner's failure
to declare whether or not Litvinenko had
been murdered, he dedicated himself to
finding the murderer. Does that sound as
wacky to you as it does to me?

A Stacked Deck

This coroner's case was seeming to me more
and more like a lame attempt to hold a
kangaroo court.

The oddest thing about it is that a coroner's
inquest is not legally supposed to be a court
to find culpability. British law actually
forbids it from doing so. Something was
really wrong here. And nobody was noticing
it.

That's when I decided that something

needed to be done about the suspicious way the case was being handled. People were inexplicably being fed a phony bill of goods about the Litvinenko matter. And the case was spilling over into international politics. Adversarial rhetoric between world powers was intensifying. If this continued to escalate, who knows where these tensions could lead?

I felt compelled to take this on and try to fight the widespread fabrications that were being accepted worldwide as facts. Something had to be done to counter the direction things were taking. So I began a process of intervention.

Chapter 5
The Intervention

Success! But sadly no follow-up.

THE objective here was to end the malicious witch hunt for Russian state culpability. This was no attempt to thwart justice. If actual evidence were to have turned up it would change my perception of things completely.

But a paramount problem here is that almost everyone was being taken in by the fabricated mainstream story about Litvinenko.

I gave considerable study to the techniques that were used in concocting and propagating the false story. I wanted to know what accounted for the specious story being so believable.

The answer I found, in part, is a phenomenon known as "confirmation bias." This is a psychological term for people's tendency to interpret information in ways that are partial to their existing beliefs, expectations, or hypotheses.

There's something more, though. The false

narrative also invokes the use of archetypes, i.e., concepts that are universally imbedded in individual psyches. Litvinenko was characterized as a hero, a dissident. Putin was painted as a devil. Jungian psychologist Dr. Brian A. Shaw examined the story and concurred that it has been built through the use of common archetypes.

(A more in-depth treatment of confirmation bias and the use of archetypes is given in my book *Ukraine in the Crosshairs*.)

But the short of it all is that the persistent campaign to claim Russian culpability in the Litvinenko case was being orchestrated with smoke and mirrors. That's what needed to be stopped. That's why an intervention was needed.

Throughout this intervention I was aided directly by a senior British law expert, a well-connected Russian journalist, and, of course, my own staff. A number of others played key and influential roles at various points along the way.

The steps we took to counteract the powerful media blitz and trumped-up story, in the end, turned out to win supreme. The British witch hunt for Russian state culpability was pulled back. Now official London was finally rejecting the nonsense that had prevailed for so long. What we had done succeeded.

The Road to Success

A number of people have asked me how we were able to manage such a turnabout. That's a question that is difficult to answer. It was a very intricate process. And it involved the cooperation of people whose identities are best kept confidential.

What's more, I'm unwilling, based on past experience, to make this process sound like it is a blueprint that just anyone could implement.

Once I made the mistake of revealing a variant of this methodology when there was a need to solve a different problem. But then some idea-poachers who neither fully understood the situation nor had the skills for implementing the plan came along. What they lacked in know-how, they made up for in financial resources. They took the basic plan, tried to implement it themselves, and ended up failing miserably. And in doing so they worsened the situation. That ultimately made solving the problem more difficult and more costly.

I'll tell you of the specific instance I'm thinking of:

The Berezovsky-NSC Caper

In 2001 the *Washington Post* published a letter from Berezovsky. In it he proposed a plan for remediating Russia's press freedom problems. His reasoning was based on a fabricated description of the state of affairs. He was likely angling for something that would ultimately benefit him in some way. In fact, he was asking for millions of American dollars.

The *Post* later printed my response. In it I described an alternate solution I had been developing, one based on realities, practicalities, and sound economics. In other venues I later elaborated on that plan.

Well, it seems that the White House National Security Council liked my plan. But they thought they might just as well implement it themselves.

Right from the start it was apparent to me

that they had neither the relevant insights nor skills for carrying out such a plan. But they went ahead anyway. They took the plan and ran with it.

There was a lot of publicity forthcoming about the NSC initiative. Much of the implementation responsibility was passed on to the State Department.

Its press release said that the National Association of Broadcasters and the Newspaper Association of America had approached the US government with a desire to help the Russian media. They wanted to promote true press freedom in Russia, it said.

A Governmental Fraud Ensues

I called those organizations and asked what the story was behind that press release. What they told me was enlightening. They said that they, the organizations, had been contacted by the State Department, not vice versa, and were invited to put their names to a program. But they were still waiting to learn what it was all about and what was expected of them. Basically they were in the dark.

The US organizations, according to this NSC plan, were to work with Russian counterpart organizations, and to jointly push for remediating Russia's media woes.

This sounded really strange. That's because Russia had no counterparts to those influential American media organizations. Hmmm. The Russian media organizations were weak and lacking influence.

Armed with that, I called the State Department official designated by NSC as the point of contact. I asked her about the program. She simply regurgitated the press release, and reiterated the claim that the government had been approached by the American professional organizations.

I told her I had just talked with representatives of those organizations. They told me, I said, that they had not contacted the US government about the matter, and that this very same State Department representative that I was talking to had contacted them in the first place. That representative, without missing a beat, said, "Well that is correct." In other words it was a flat admission that the State Department story was a complete fabrication.

Responding to the State Department's Fraud

I hired an assistant to help salvage matters. She was a former CIA officer who had considerable background in Russian affairs. The job I gave her was to try assisting NSC to reorient its program along more practical and honest lines, or if that couldn't be worked out, to somehow scuttle the NSC project to keep it from doing more damage.

She tried hard to talk sense to the State Department officials both in Washington and Moscow. From what I could see, neither they nor the NSC were at all open to outside input. Yet they seemed to have no idea how much they did not know about Russia's media milieu.

With White House backing, this project had access to all the right people. Representatives from American and Russian organizations met numerous times to hammer out a plan to help the Russian media. A summit was arranged for them to present their findings at a meeting in Moscow with the Russian and American presidents. Wow, what an audience!

What did they tell the presidents? It was that they could not achieve a consensus and had nothing substantive to report.

That should not have been surprising. The basic premise for this effort included several outright myths: (1) that the American organizations had any understanding of the very peculiar Russian media sector, (2) that Russian media matters would be of any real consequence to the American organizations; and (3) that the initiative for the project came from the American organizations, when in reality it was an NSC plot, the purpose of which defies any reasonable understanding.

Where did the project end up? After the fiasco of gaining the ears of the Russian and American presidents and telling them they couldn't agree, what happened? My assistant asked if she could contact "her boys" to see what could be done about this troubled US initiative. Of course, I acquiesced.

Well, basically, the project ended up collapsing of its own dysfunction. There were still budget funds remaining. So the Russian participants were sent at US taxpayer expense on junkets to New Orleans and Las

Vegas. I hope that a good time was had by all. Cheers!

So now I think you might understand my refusal to divulge much detail about how to remediate Russia's current reputational problems regarding the Litvinenko case and others.

We all should try to protect against idiotic idea-poachers, especially bureaucratic ones.

The Litvinenko Remediation Project

Despite the foregoing, the challenge remains of how to explain the efficacy of the Litvinenko project we undertook to call off the specious hunt for Russian state culpability.

For the purpose of giving some insight into the overall methodology, I decided to give the process a name.

I'm calling this methodology "Surgical Solution of Practical Problems."

It's simply a name I invented. It is a general approach to solving problems, and its utility is by far not applicable exclusively to the

Litvinenko case.

Not SOP But SSOPP

SSOPP is the acronym for the Surgical Solution of Practical Problems. In a sense the methodology is like a non-military counterpart to a surgical air strike.

It uses a proprietary skill set for resolving critically important problems. It does that by directly intervening in undesirable situations that require a positive solution. SSOPP is particularly well suited for achieving a well-defined objective in the international relations arena.

The SSOPP approach is not formulaic. It does not involve traditional diplomacy.

SOP is the acronym for standard operating procedure. But SSOPP is the antithesis of that. It has no pre-structured agenda. Instead it utilizes a strategy-agile methodology to adapt itself to each application, to respond effectively to unfolding developments, and to build upon responses from the problem source to our intervention initiatives.

In the Litvinenko intervention, the general components included:

1. Identifying the problem source as anyone involved at the source in advancing or validating fabricated stories of Russian state culpability.

2. Surveying vulnerabilities of the problem source.

3. Focusing on the vulnerability most useful for effectuating change.

4. Characterizing that vulnerability in a way that disadvantages the problem source.

5. Using a combination of direct communication with the problem source and with those that have practical control over the problem source.

6. Supporting those initiatives with media releases, articles, and interviews.

7. Utilizing strategies that are superior to those used by the problem source.

8. Outsmarting the problem source.

9. Maneuvering the problem source or its overseers into a position wherein capitulation will be the most self-serving alternative.

In the Litvinenko case the most useful vulnerability was that the coroner was pursuing the case in a way that was at variance with the intricacies of British law. In effect he was not performing his statutory duties.

We characterized the coroner as a rogue operator who was refusing to do his job.

This SSOPP project involved over fifty interactions with key British officials and the publication of dozens of media articles.

In the end, the coroner was ordered by the Home Secretary to stop his witch hunt for Russian state culpability and instead to perform his statutory duty to determine the manner and cause of death.

The Home Secretary had embraced the argument that we had singularly been making throughout the intervention. In the end she bought into the position that we uniquely had presented.

The SSOPP intervention was halted at that point. It had served its purpose of creating a successful work- product example. Key stake holders were invited to support a continuation of the work. None stepped forth, however. Sadly the success of the intervention was ultimately wasted by this lack of follow-up.

Epilogue

Funny thing, though. The methodology we used in the Litvinenko case could also have been applied to other fabricated assaults against Russia and its leader. In the years following Litvinenko's death there were many. Georgia and the Sochi Olympics, just to mention two.

"Russia without Spin" (www.russiawithoutspin.com), a project that I strongly support, has in the past repeatedly proposed applying an SSOPP-type methodology for addressing the multitude of Russia's international reputational problems. It has yet to receive a positive response from the key governmental and multinational commercial stakeholders, however. Perhaps the successful work-product example of the Litvinenko case

intervention will promote a more receptive
future response.

Chapter 6
Live Reports Since 2011

Articles that chronicle the evolution of the case.

WHAT follows are over 30 articles I authored and a few media interviews I granted. They all relate to the Litvinenko case in some way. Since the articles were written as stand-alone pieces, you will find some repetition.

The articles show their dates of publication. This will enable you to appreciate the unfolding developments as they appeared along the way.

The Who-Done-It Fraud
January 20, 2012

Is this a quest to make a hoax look real?
Was Litvinenko really murdered?

The ubiquitous "who murdered Alexander Litvinenko" news story has turned out to be a fraud.

In late 2006, world media outlets were reporting that the former KGB spy was murdered on orders of Vladimir Putin. It was one of the biggest, most sensational news stories of the time. Now a new video turns that account upside down.

The video shows that Litvinenko wasn't a spy, he never worked for the KGB, and the claim that Vladimir Putin ordered the murder is not fact-based. It was merely an allegation made by an arch-enemy of Putin's. What's more, the London coroner hasn't ever concluded that Litvinenko was even murdered.

The widely-disseminated news stories about Litvinenko don't match the facts. The stories appear to have been fabricated.

A video titled *The Who-Done-It Fraud* is the
first in a series of supplements to my recent
book entitled *The Phony Litvinenko Murder*.
The book examines the media coverage of
the purported poisoning of Litvinenko by
radioactive polonium.

The new video presents actual, rarely-heard
audio recordings of Litvinenko himself,
speaking from his hospital bed less than 2
weeks before his death. In it he clearly
suggests who he believes poisoned him --
and it isn't Putin. Also on the video is an
exclusive recording of a close associate of
Litvinenko who backs up Litvinenko's belief
about his poisoner.

The video traces the strange odyssey of the
changing stories told by the media about
who was responsible for the poisoning. First
the media reports accused one person, then
another, and then still another. But the
media never explained why their accusations
were shifting.

Certainly there must be some significance to
why the identity of the accused person has
mysteriously shifted. But media reports
didn't dig into that mystery. They just
ignored this very significant aspect of the

case. Was that a result of widespread journalistic incompetence? Or was there something sinister behind the curious nature of the media reports? We're just left to wonder.

But the real kicker in the story is this:

It's not even certain that Alexander Litvinenko was actually murdered!

That's right. The London Coroner never ruled the death to be a homicide. *The Who-Done-It Fraud* video presents exclusive confirmation of this, direct from the coroner's office.

But the worldwide media have been mum on that issue, too.

In fact, the world media outlets were initially very quiet about the Litvinenko story altogether. Litvinenko was apparently poisoned on November 1, 2006. The BBC Russian Service ran the story on November 11, in its transmissions aimed at Russia's population. But there was nary a word about the case back home in London. Other British media weren't covering it either. Isn't that puzzling? The poisoning happened in

London. Litvinenko was a British citizen. We know from the BBC Russian Service report that at least someone in the British media knew about the story. But there was no coverage.

It could be because Litvinenko just wasn't considered newsworthy. After all, his name wasn't exactly a household word at that time. Few people around the globe really knew who he was, much less cared. So perhaps the decision not to cover the poisoning of an unknown actually represented good journalistic judgment.

That all changed around November 19, however. News of the Litvinenko poisoning began bursting out all around the world. The Who-Done-It Fraud video explores this phenomenon, and suggests a foreshadowing event that may have been the game changer.

But come to think of it, if Litvinenko was basically not newsworthy, why was there such an enormous eruption of interest that late in the game?

Media outlets called the case a James Bond mystery. But to me, their coverage was more like *Alice in Wonderland*: a fantasy adventure filled with illogical nonsense, and without a factual basis. The underlying premises of the media coverage just don't hold up to scrutiny.

The Who-Done-It Fraud video can be viewed at www.OmnicomPress.com/plmv1 or on YouTube.com.

The Russian Spy Story Unraveled
February 20, 2012

It turns out Litvinenko never was a spy!

The worldwide media have been caught fabricating facts in the Alexander Litvinenko spy story. A new video shows that the famous spy never was a spy.

But in late 2006, reports naming Litvinenko a former spy were big headlines. World media outlets were reporting that the former KGB spy was murdered on orders of Vladimir Putin.

The Russian Spy Story Unraveled video is the second in a series of supplements to my recent book entitled *The Phony Litvinenko Murder*. The book examines the media coverage of the purported poisoning of Litvinenko by radioactive polonium.

In the new video, a list of famous Russian spies is presented. Litvinenko stands out as the only one whose spy status was never reliably affirmed. Indeed, two sources have come forth contradicting the media's spy assertion. They explain that Litvinenko's security service job involved working against organized crime in Russia. He wasn't a spy, and didn't work for the KGB. In my book I present details of this from a well-informed, former instructor at the FSB Academy. The FSB is Russia's security service. Now in the new video, you can hear this directly from Litvinenko's widow, in her own words.

Nonetheless, media outlets insisted that Litvinenko was a spy. Typical headlines included:

--Ex-KGB spy 'poisoned by alpha radiation'
--Mysterious case of the poisoned spy
--Ex-KGB agent's poisoning echoes Cold War plot
--Radiation Poisoning Killed Ex-Russian Spy

I asked the media outlets behind each headline why they called Litvinenko a spy? They all refused to answer.

Another noteworthy headline said:

--Litvinenko spy story could be acted out by Johnny Depp

So on top of all the specious media coverage,

it appears that a movie may be produced about a spy who wasn't a spy.

That's fitting, in a sense. Depp previously starred in the Walt Disney production of *Alice in Wonderland*. Like Alice, the Litvinenko story told by the media seems to be a fantasy adventure filled with illogical nonsense, as well. The basic premise of the story, that Litvinenko was a former spy, seems to lack a factual basis. It is a concoction. The media reports just don't hold up to scrutiny.

The Russian Spy Story Unraveled video can be viewed at www.OmnicomPress.com/plmv2 or on YouTube.com.

The Faked Deathbed Statement
March 24, 2012

Who really wrote it?

News outlets reported that from his deathbed, reputed former spy Alexander Litvinenko accused Russian president Vladimir Putin of poisoning him.

But there is one very big thing wrong with that story. The news media had no factual basis for it. The story was absolutely fabricated. In fact, a culprit has come forward and confessed that it was he, not Litvinenko, who wrote the so-called deathbed statement.

The Deathbed Statement -- Who Really Wrote It? is the third in a series of supplements to my recent book entitled *The Phony Litvinenko Murder*. The book examines the media coverage of the purported poisoning of Litvinenko by radioactive polonium.

This new video offers recorded proof from Litvinenko himself that flatly dispels the specious media reports on the deathbed statement.

The Deathbed Statement -- Who Really Wrote It? video can be viewed at www.OmnicomPress.com/plmv3 or on YouTube.com.

Gorbuntsov Case is No Litvinenko Story
March 30, 2012

Tone of media reports suggest recent London killing fits that pattern of Litvinenko's death.

A recent *Guardian* story was headlined, "Attack on Russian banker in London leaves trail of clues back to Moscow." Doesn't that sound reminiscent of many media reports in the Alexander Litvinenko poisoning?

In that case the "trail of clues" was radioactive. Literally! It involved radioactive polonium, a substance widely reported to have been responsible for Litvinenko's death. And the media allegations of who was behind the poisoning were explosive. They alleged the culprit was Russian president Vladimir Putin.

The *Guardian* story reports on the recent shooting in London of a former Russian bank owner, a man named German Gorbuntsov. He has been living in London since 2010, the reports say.

The Gorbuntsov story's similarity to the Litvinenko case seems to stop with that *Guardian* headline. As suggestive it might sound of Kremlin involvement, this story's text makes no such allegation. That's a refreshing change of pace from the usual Litvinenko coverage. It was, and still is, replete with unfounded allegations, explanations that don't make sense, and conflicting information.

My book, *The Phony Litvinenko Murder*, thoroughly debunks the troubled media coverage of the case. In a new supplementary video, I question the authenticity of Litvinenko's well-publicized deathbed statement. You can see that video at www.omnicompress.com/plmv3.

The Litvinenko Contamination Case is Contaminated
April 21, 2012

It's ironic that a story about a death from radioactive contamination has itself become contaminated. But this time it's from harmful misinformation.

Why is the 2006 poisoning death of Alexander Litvinenko still unsolved today? Is it likely this high-profile case may never be solved?

Mention the Alexander Litvinenko case, and people think of radioactive contamination. Now, though, it's looking like the case itself has become contaminated.

The London coroner's office has played a central role in the Litvinenko case. But these days it appears to be in disarray and hiding from the public.

What's Behind This?

While researching my book, *The Phony Litvinenko Murder*, I broke the news that the coroner never had concluded that

Litvinenko was murdered. All those media reports that said he was are simply unfounded speculation. Details are in the book.

No credible explanation has been given as to what really happened to Litvinenko. Why didn't the coroner wrap up the case years ago? Until last fall, there was just dead silence from the coroner.

The first sign of life came in fall 2011. That's when the coroner announced that finally an inquest would be held. It took place on October 13, 2011. No, it wasn't Friday the 13th; it was a Thursday. But given all the events that followed, it might as well have been a Friday the 13th. It's that strange.

After that inquest, coroner Dr. Andrew Reid issued an official statement that begins: "Following the pre-inquest review held today at St Pancreas Coroners Court I would like to confirm that I am yet to provide a written ruling to the properly interested persons and potential properly interested persons. Therefore I have indicated my preliminary view that there should be further investigations into the wider circumstances about which allegations were made at the hearings today."

What did he just say? The statement certainly is not written in plain English.

As an aside, I ran a Fog Index calculation on his whole statement. I publish *Editors Only* (www.editorsonly.com), a monthly for magazine editors. We often pick passages from magazines or newspapers for Fog analysis. It is a measure of how readable copy is. Reid's statement has a Fog Index of over 25. That number tells how many years of formal education are needed to understand it. Shakespeare, Mark Twain, and the *Bible* average around 6. Publications like *Time* and the *Wall Street Journal* come in around 11. This article up to the Reid quote scores about 10. At over 25, Reid's statement seems unnecessarily complex. Was he trying to be obfuscatory?

Two things that can be gleaned: The inquest wasn't really an inquest. Now Reid calls it a pre-inquest. He said allegations were made by someone during the pre-inquest. But Reid didn't say what they were.

He goes on to textually mumble about possibly bumping the case to a higher judicial official. Reid also suggests he's still awaiting a further decision from the prosecutor. It's about Litvinenko's death. But he doesn't tell more. He then says he's interested in the outcome of an appeals court matter. It apparently involves some people connected with the Litvinenko case. But Reid doesn't provide the who or the what.

Then, in a Friday-the-13th-weird series of events, (1) Reid calls for MI5 and MI6 to release secret documents about Litvinenko (January 28 -- http://bit.ly/Jp21gR), (2) Reid is hospitalized for appendicitis (January 31 -- BSR-Russia, no longer in print), and (3) Reid is removed from all cases amidst surprising allegations that he had hired his wife back in 2009 (February 9 -- http://bit.ly/I29cKl).

It Adds Up To...

So what we have is a coroner's office that after five years hasn't been able to make up its mind about what happened to Litvinenko. Then, when Coroner Reid finally gets off the dime and calls for secret files on Litvinenko to be opened, he suddenly is hospitalized for appendicitis. And next, without skipping a beat, supposed dirt on him dating back three years is dug up and he's abruptly removed from the case.

Whatever Reid had started, he wasn't going to be allowed to finish.

After several tries at asking the coroner's press office to explain what really happened to Reid, no answers were forthcoming. A journalist I know who called seeking to interview Reid was told that Reid is persona non grata. Indeed!

If the coroner's office were finally to render a verdict about Litvinenko's death, who would believe it? By its own bumbling actions, the office has earned itself an Inspector Clouseau image. It has indeed contaminated the Litvinenko contamination case. It's hard to imagine how the officials could explain their way out of this one.

Another Contamination Source

The folly of the coroner's office isn't the only contamination of the case, though. There's also the way in which the media have confounded any attempt by the public to achieve an accurate understanding of what happened.

The media story about Alexander Litvinenko, in a nutshell, is this: Former KGB Spy Litvinenko was murdered by Russian president Vladimir Putin who poisoned him with radioactive polonium.

But if you look for the facts behind those allegations, you come to realize that none of that story may be true. Indeed, it really appears to be a sheer fabrication propagated by the media.

Not one aspect of that media story has a basis in fact.

The Real Story

In my research, I found evidence that Litvinenko

--did not work for the KGB, and

--he never was a spy.

I produced a video short about this. It's called *The Russian Spy Story Unraveled*. It is a free supplement to my book, *The Phony Litvinenko Murder* (www.OmnicomPress.com/plm). You can see the video here:

www.OmnicomPress.com/plmv2.

Another troubling media issue concerns who was responsible for Litvinenko's death. First the news named Italian Mario Scaramella as the poisoner. Then it switched to Vladimir Putin. And finally it named Andrei Lugovoi who presumably did it on behalf of Putin.

Many news accounts described Lugovoi simply as a Russian businessman. Some say he was former KGB. But it's significant that he worked for Berezovsky during the 1990s. That gets little media attention.

The crux of the news stories is that close associates of Putin picked Lugovoi, a man who had been closely associated with Putin arch-enemy Berezovsky, to assassinate Litvinenko in London. I don't know if any of that is true. But, let's assume for a moment that it is. Why didn't the media at least remark upon the incongruity of picking and trusting someone associated with Putin's enemies to pull off a volatile, covert, murderous mission?

I did another video, this time on that topic. It's called *The Who Done It Fraud*, again, a supplement to my book. You can see the video here: www.OmnicomPress.com/plmv1.

The media nonsense about Litvinenko goes on to hit another low, and now it's on the widely-reported deathbed statement. You may recall that this was a written statement that mysteriously appeared right after Litvinenko's death. Explosively, it named Russian president Vladimir Putin as his poisoner.

But that was a real switcheroo. Earlier the media reported that Litvinenko believed he was poisoned by Mario Scaramella. Litvinenko disclosed that in a November 11, 2006 interview broadcast by BBC. On American TV, Yuri Felshtinsky who co-wrote with Litvinenko a book about terrorism in Russia, said Litvinenko told him he was sure it was Mario Scaramella that did it.

The switcheroo first surfaced in media reports almost a week before Litvinenko's death. They said Litvinenko had fingered Russian president Vladimir Putin. But, the media weren't quoting Litvinenko himself. Instead their source was Boris Berezovsky, a British tycoon who is a fugitive from Russia, his former homeland. But no media outlets seemed to have heard this directly from

Litvinenko.

The next shoe dropped when Litvinenko died. In the so-called deathbed statement, Litvinenko himself spoke out to the world to accuse Putin. Media accounts said Litvinenko dictated the statement in his own words. But later it comes out that he didn't! The statement was written by someone else and was passed off as something of Litvinenko's. You can see my video on this slice of the case here: www.OmnicomPress.com/plmv3.

Are you getting a clearer picture of just how completely contaminated this case is?

It Gets Even Stranger

Just when you think the Litvinenko case couldn't become more contaminated, it does.

Recently Litvinenko's brother, Maxim, challenged the media's non-fact-based claims about polonium. This took place in an interview on Russian TV. Maxim asserts that the lab tests that found polonium in Alexander's urine were rigged. Maxim said that polonium was somehow introduced into Litvinenko's urine specimen that went out for testing. That would mean Litvinenko may not have died of polonium contamination.

But, Maxim didn't offer any facts to back up his story. So I wrote to the coroner's office seeking clarification: "In a recent interview Maxim Litvinenko, brother of Alexander Litvinenko, suggests that polonium detected in Alexander's urine was a result of deliberate contamination of the urine bag below his bed. Does the coroner's office have any information that would conflict with that allegation? I'd be grateful for your clarification. Thanks."

The reply?

"We do not have a comment on this. We are awaiting an inquest date."

Oh, another inquest? I followed up: "Thank you. When do you expect the inquest to take place? Who will be convening it?"

The answer?

"The coroner has appointed a legal team of solicitors and counsel. Further hearing dates will follow and properly interested persons and media will be notified in due course."

So Reid has been off the case since February 9, and they're still thinking about what to do next in this November 2006 case! Does this sound as fishy to you as it does to me? Are they trying to hide something?

In any event, the credibility of the coroner's office seems to have been irreparably damaged regarding Litvinenko. How can the case ever be solved in a way that is believable?

What's more, there are now many entrenched and vested interests with a stake in maintaining the illusions perpetuated by all the nonsensical news stories. Very conspicuous leaders in the UK and the US have taken strong positions based on those fallacious reports. These powerful people will look mighty foolish if no legitimate evidence is ever found and presented to support the "Putin did it" scenario.

Is that a reason why the London Coroner's office seems to be in such disarray? Is it why the officials seem so unwilling to provide clear and responsive answers?

I don't know if it is. But the whole Litvinenko case seems to have become too contaminated by the nonsensical fantasy of the media reports and the folly of the coroner's office.

Together they've reduced the matter to nothing more than a fantasy adventure with Litvinenko playing the role of Alice in Wonderland and the coroner's office filling in as Inspector Clouseau.

A Costly Folly
May 21, 2012

The fanciful Litvinenko case isn't coming cheap.

Londoners are being asked to foot the $7 million bill for the dead-end Litvinenko death probe.

"EXCLUSIVE: Town Hall stunned by £1m bill to hold inquest into death of poisoned former KGB agent," shouted the lead headline in a recent *Camden New Journal*. Camden is a tiny borough, a constituent part of the City of London. One million pounds, or about $1.5 million, would be its share of what's expected to be a yearlong inquest into Alexander Litvinenko's death. Borough leaders fear that the cost of the Litvinenko case will take money away from important public services and school repairs.

But the newspaper's story missed the real headline here: No official certification has ever been issued as to the cause and manner of death. So it's not certain his death was a homicide or that it was polonium that killed him.

That means Camden's money will go to determine who did it, before it has even been concluded what was done! That's the big story here. Why would anyone want to pay such a high price for that kind of nonsense?

What's more, if the coroner were to finally issue a verdict on who or what was responsible for the death after these five and a half long years, who would believe it? There have been too many suspicious circumstances.

--Why has it taken so long?

--What's really behind the fate of former coroner Andrew Reid? Just last January he finally asked MI5/MI6 to release information about the Litvinenko case. Then he was reportedly hospitalized for appendicitis. And soon thereafter he was removed from all cases amidst surprising allegations that he had hired his wife back in 2009. Why was that just coming up now?

--Remember also the notorious deathbed accusation that Vladimir Putin was behind the poisoning. It turns out it was written by someone else and misrepresented to be Litvinenko's own words.

I detailed yet more of the nonsense surrounding the Litvinenko case in my book, *The Phony Litvinenko Murder*.

The *Camden New Journal* even reported that in 2008 someone tried to burn down the hospital building in which Litvinenko had been treated. Sniffer dogs discovered three "fire accelerators" planted in the basement. How weird is that?

It's hard to imagine how this case can ever be solved satisfactorily. But it looks like someone will be footing the $7 million bill for continuing the nonsense.

Magnitsky Bill Drags Senators into Foreign Plot
June 27, 2012

Here's another misinformation campaign a la Litvinenko.

Senators are pressing ahead with the "Magnitsky Bill," seemingly oblivious that they've been hoodwinked by foreign agitators whose aims are served by the bill. The legislation is ostensibly about the 2009 death of Russian Sergei Magnitsky. He was denied medical treatment for his illnesses while in pre-trial detention. His arrest had been in connection with a large tax-evasion case. The bill would inflict punishment upon the Russian officials who were complicit in the death.

However, the bill sets out to do a job that's already been done. The Obama administration claims it has already taken punitive action against those Russian officials.

The legislation seems to allege that Magnitsky's death was a human rights abuse, representative of the intentional policies and practices of the Russian state. But, the facts refute that allegation. The Kremlin's own Human Rights Council reported that Magnitsky had been murdered. The death was called a tragedy by Vladimir Putin. Dmitry Medvedev fired a number of top local and federal prison officials. The Russian government continues to seek a full accounting of the corruption and malfeasance that led to Magnitsky's death.

Given the foregoing, the Magnitsky bill is clearly neither a necessary nor constructive action to support human rights in Russia. The bill seems to be a trumped-up cause that is the product of an international effort to destabilize Russia. It in fact is not an American bill. The Magnitsky bill follows a template provided by foreign agitators who appear to be seeking destabilization and deligitimization in Russia. This foreign effort has resulted in similar legislation being introduced in multiple countries around the world. That's even been acknowledged by some members of Congress.

Destabilizing Russia is not in the interests of the Russian people. It also is not in the interests of the United States. Alienating Russia will compromise burgeoning

American business interests there. It will also disadvantage US diplomatic efforts to "reset" the relationship between the two countries.

This Magnitsky disinformation caper is reminiscent of the trap Congress fell into over the Alexander Litvinenko case. In 2007, Congresswoman Ileana Ros-Lehtinen (R-FL) introduced legislation accusing the Russian government of poisoning reputed former KGB spy Alexander Litvinenko in London. News reports had quoted a deathbed statement by Litvinenko that fingered Russian president Vladimir Putin. The only trouble is that the whole murder story was a fabrication. I wrote a book titled *The Phony Litvinenko Murder*. In it I show that Litvinenko was not a spy, and he never worked for the KGB. What's more, the London Coroner never deemed his death to be a homicide. The deathbed statement turned out to be a fake. A former Soviet citizen later confessed that it was he who wrote the words, not Litvinenko. He also admitted there was no evidence to back up his accusation against Putin. It turns out the fake story had been perpetrated by a wealthy arch-enemy of Putin's. But Congress swallowed it all hook, line, and sinker.

It looks like members of the US Senate now have been tricked into supporting another foreign initiative that would have negative consequences for the United States.

I sought comment from two Senators caught up in the fiasco. Sen. Richard Blumenthal is my senator here in Connecticut. He's also a co-sponsor of the Magnitsky Bill. But when I asked his office to comment, the staffers told me they didn't want to talk about it. It was a strange response to give a constituent. I also contacted the office of Sen. Jim Webb (D-VA). He's a member of the Foreign Relations Committee, and was responsible for the bill's consideration being put off until June 26. His office not only wouldn't comment, but wouldn't even explain why Webb had asked for the delay. There doesn't seem to be much transparency surrounding this legislation.

The Magnitsky Bill (S-1039) was introduced by Sen. Benjamin Cardin (D-MD) and has the following co-sponsors:

Kelly Ayotte, R-NH; Mark Begich, D-AK; Richard Blumenthal, D-CT; Roy Blunt, R-MO; Barbara Boxer, D-CA; Sherrod Brown, D-OH; Richard Burr, R-NC; Robert P. Casey, Jr. D-PA; Tom Coburn, R-OK; Susan M.

Collins, R-ME; Christopher A. Coons, D-DE; John Cornyn, R-TX; Jim DeMint, R-SC; Richard Durbin, D-IL; Lindsey Graham, R-SC; Tom Harkin, D-IA; James M. Inhofe, R-OK; Mike Johanns, R-NE; Ron Johnson, R-WI; Mark Steven Kirk, R-IL; Jon Kyl, R-AZ; Mike Lee, R-UT; Joseph I Lieberman,. I-CT; John McCain, R-AZ; Robert Menendez, D-NJ; James E. Risch, R-ID; Marco Rubio, R-FL; Charles E Schumer,. D-NY; Jeff Sessions, R-AL; Jeanne Shaheen, D-NH; John Thune, R-SD; Tom Udall, D-NM; Sheldon Whitehouse, D-RI; Roger F. Wicker, R-MS; Ron Wyden, R-OR.

I wonder if any of them will do their own homework on this bill, realize what they've fallen into, and have the courage to get out before the damage is done.

Al-Jazeera, Others Spread Counterfactual Stories about Litvinenko, Arafat
August 20, 2012

And the misinformation campaigns keep on coming. The media must think the public will be fooled by anything.

The Yasser Arafat story that broke in July brought on a new wave of incessant references to Alexander Litvinenko's alleged murder by polonium in 2006. The Arafat reports went viral in the mainstream press and social media. Al-Jazeera seems to have been at the source of them all. It was trumpeting the discovery of polonium contamination on the garments Arafat wore near the time of death. Al-Jazeera was suggesting that Arafat like Litvinenko could have been poisoned.

Here's what Al-Jazeera was saying about Litvinenko: "Polonium was used to kill Alexander Litvinenko, a onetime Russian spy turned dissident."

Well, that flies in the face of the facts. Back

in October 2011, while researching my book, *The Phony Litvinenko Murder* (www.omnicompress.com/plm), I sought official confirmation of my understanding of the case. My research was indicating that the London Coroner hadn't ever concluded that Litvinenko was murdered or that polonium poisoning was the cause of death. So I asked for verification. The coroner's office wrote back: "That is correct, William. Thanks for seeking clarification."

When I started seeing all the Al-Jazeera and copycat stories in July, I thought that perhaps something had changed. Did the coroner recently conclude that Litvinenko had been murdered and that polonium was the cause of death? So, I questioned the coroner's office again:

"Has the coroner issued a finding on the cause and manner of death of Alexander Litvinenko? My understanding has been that no such finding has been reached. But world media, in connection with the recent stories about Yasser Arafat, have been widely reporting that polonium was used to murder Litvinenko. Thus I am interested in knowing if the coroner has made a determination of the cause and manner of death in the

Litvinenko case."

The answer came back: no new determination. So the authoritative word is still the same. No murder, no polonium, still to this day. But Al-Jazeera was continuing to issue its counterfactual news stories. That made me wonder if anything Al-Jazeera was reporting in its Arafat stories is correct.

According to French news agency AFP, "On Tuesday [July 3], Al-Jazeera television broadcast the results of a nine-month probe it commissioned into the 2004 death of the veteran Palestinian leader that indicated he could have been poisoned with the radioactive substance polonium."

That report also said the polonium had been detected at the Institute of Radiation Physics in Switzerland, where Arafat's clothing had been sent for testing. I found a copy of the report and a related press release. They don't say what Al-Jazeera says they say. The report seems to heap evidence on an opposite conclusion.

Al-Jazeera says the report indicated Arafat "may have been poisoned with polonium." But the Institute of Radiation Physics says the polonium detected is "not sufficient to determine the causes of death." It adds that "some of the findings in the forensic report are inconsistent with an acute radiation syndrome."

Did Al-Jazeera misunderstand the report? Or is it trying to put one over on its audience?

There's something else Al-Jazeera got wrong about Litvinenko. Its reports called him a "onetime Russian spy turned dissident." I offer evidence in my book that he never was a spy and hadn't worked for the KGB. And calling him a dissident? When I hear "Russian dissident" I think of Solzhenitsyn, Sakharov, and Bonner. They are well-recognized Russian dissidents. Litvinenko had been quite a critic of Putin, and many media reports claimed Putin put out orders to kill him. My book shows that was all trumped-up. To put Litvinenko in the same category as Solzhenitsyn et al is just plain nonsense.

Originally, I toyed with calling this article, "Who Framed Vladimir Putin." A 1988 film called "Who Framed Roger Rabbit" inspired the idea. In that movie, cartoon characters interacted with real people in a who-done-it fantasy comedy. That's the same situation that Putin is in these days. Except there isn't anything funny about it. The media have become the cartoon characters here. They've failed in their responsibility to be reliable reporters of fact-based news.

Recent Update: On March 17, 2015 Associated Press reported: "French experts have ruled out the theory that radioactive polonium poisoning caused the death of Palestinian leader Yasser Arafat in 2004. The Nanterre prosecutor said in a communique Monday that there were no traces of polonium 210 in Arafat's urine during his stay at a French military hospital prior to his death, and that any traces of the substance recorded after his exhumation were 'of an environmental origin' in the tomb."

Does Pussy Riot News Story Have Hidden Agenda?
September 5, 2012

Another hunt to bag Vladimir Putin.

The Pussy Riot news story may be nothing more than a ploy to compromise the Russian state. Eerie similarities exist with the famous Alexander Litvinenko case from 2006.

The Pussy Riot story portrayed in the press gives no obvious hint of the ploy. Reports suggest that Pussy Riot is a group of principled dissidents standing up for free speech and opposing Putin's oppression. A well-known American university professor wrote an article likening the Pussy Riot group to Dostoyevsky. He said the members represent "a long-standing tradition of dissent by the Russian intelligentsia."

That professor and the Western media must have a strange concept of "intelligentsia." Nadezhda Tolokonnikova is regarded by many as the leader of Pussy Riot. Nude photos of that intelligentsia member are widely displayed across the Internet. The *Guardian* newspaper claims she was "taking part in an orgy in Moscow's biological museum." Other stunts reported to be associated with the Pussy Riot group also involved indecency and lasciviousness.

But this darker side of the Pussy Riot group has received scant coverage in the press. Certainly that image of wanton exhibitionism would seem to contrast sharply with the dignified characterizations that have prevailed in media stories.

Media have also missed intersections between the Pussy Riot story and the fabricated media account of Alexander Litvinenko's purported murder. I wrote a book titled *The Phony Litvinenko Murder*. It shows that despite widespread media claims of Russian state involvement in Litvinenko's death, the London Coroner in fact has never even concluded he was a victim of homicide.

So, it was startling to see in media reports that people and organizations that played key roles in the fallacious Litvinenko allegations are also connected to Pussy Riot. *Wired* magazine interviewed Alex Goldfarb who it identified as "a Russian expat living in New York." Goldfarb said Pussy Riot inspired him. "The grace and courage and intelligence with which they handled themselves, is all amazing of course," he added. This is apparently the same Alex Goldfarb who is reportedly employed by Boris Berezovsky, and who served as the principal spokesperson in the fabricated media stories regarding Litvinenko. Berezovsky is a wealthy arch-enemy of Russian president Vladimir Putin's, now living in London.

Certainly that was enough to start me wondering just how many common players are involved in the Pussy Riot and Litvinenko cases. Just at that time, a colleague of mine received an email from a well-known British music agent with whom he has a business relationship. The agent reported he was contacted by the London PR firm Bell Pottinger, offering his artists "up to 100,000 euros for a statement in support of the Pussy Riot." Bell Pottinger was known in the Litvinenko case to be working on behalf of Berezovsky in support of his media assault on Putin.

Is the commonality of these players in the two seemingly disparate cases just a strange coincidence? Or are the cases both examples of the same thing: someone's organized ploy to destabilize the Russian administration? I don't know the answer to those questions. But it seems to me, this is something that the public champions of Pussy Riot and the journalists covering the story should be looking into.

How Pussy Riot and Berezovsky Plot Revolutions
September 14, 2012

Here they go again.

The Pussy Riot news story has come to resemble an information riot. The uproar pits two opposing factions: One side maintains the jail sentence handed down to the three members of the punk rock group is fair. The other views it as evidence of Kremlin suppression of free speech. Neither side seems to have put the whole picture together.

The most recent round of sensational stories misquotes my comments about self-exiled tycoon Boris Berezovsky being behind the Pussy Riot incident. Some reports claim I hold absolute proof of that. Those claims are inaccurate.

What I have noted, however, are interesting intersections between the Pussy Riot story and false media accounts claiming that Alexander Litvinenko was murdered in London in 2006 by Russian security agencies. The London Coroner has never even concluded that Litvinenko was a victim of homicide, and there is no evidence that points definitively to Russia's role in his death.

The false media stories may have been orchestrated by Berezovsky as a slap at the Russian state and its leaders. It was therefore startling to see in media reports that people and organizations that played key roles in the fallacious Litvinenko allegations are also connected to Pussy Riot.

I first saw news reports that Alexander Goldfarb, who was born in Moscow and emigrated from the Soviet Union in 1975, was supposedly involved in raising funds for Pussy Riot's defense. I recognized his name from the Litvinenko case. Author of the 2007 book *Death of a Dissident: The Poisoning of Alexander Litvinenko and the Return of the KGB* and reportedly on Berezovksy's payroll, Goldfarb was a principal spokesperson in spreading the stories of Litvinenko's supposed murder by Russian authorities.

Goldfarb told *Wired* magazine recently that Pussy Riot is an inspiration to him. "The grace and courage and intelligence with which they handled themselves is all amazing, of course," he said.

That set off my curiosity. I wondered how many common players are involved in the Pussy Riot and Litvinenko cases. Meanwhile, the London public relations firm Bell Pottinger had reportedly approached a well-known British music agent with the following proposal: If he could convince his pop star clients to make public statements in support of Pussy Riot, they would purportedly receive 100,000 euros ($129,000) in compensation. Notably, Bell Pottinger was instrumental in disseminating Litvinenko stories on behalf of Berezovsky.

Is it just a coincidence that the same two players figure in two seemingly disparate cases? Or are the cases both examples of the same phenomenon: an organized plot to discredit the Kremlin?

I don't know the answer to those questions, but it seems to me that the public champions of Pussy Riot and the journalists covering the story should earnestly be looking into that.

Pussy Riot supporters portray the punk group as legitimate dissidents who stood up for free speech and opposed Putin's oppression. Wesleyan University professor Peter Rutland likened the Pussy Riot group to 19th-century writer Fyodor Dostoevsky on these opinion pages [in the *Moscow Times*]. He said the members represent "a long-standing tradition of dissent by the Russian intelligentsia."

The gushing stories of support for Pussy Riot neglect to consider that the right to free speech is not a license to infringe on the legitimate rights of others. The US Embassy in Cairo recently issued a statement regarding a Muslim-related issue: "Respect for religious beliefs is a cornerstone of American democracy. We firmly reject the actions by those who abuse the universal right of free speech to hurt the religious beliefs of others." Shouldn't that same concept apply to Pussy Riot?

But was Pussy Riot's stunt sufficient to warrant a two-year sentence? One analyst told me that Pussy Riot "got two years for interrupting vacuum cleaning at the cathedral." If that's the case, it might have been more productive to sentence them to community service, perhaps vacuuming churches themselves. That would have given them an opportunity to learn some respect for others.

Yet there is still one remaining common theme between the Pussy Riot and Litvinenko cases that is troubling. Berezovsky has not hidden his intent to foment a revolution in Russia. I've always suspected that the fabricated Litvinenko story fits into that scheme somehow.

At the same time, Nadezhda Tolokonnikova, who is considered the leader of Pussy Riot, and her husband, Pyotr Verzilov, have also told the media that revolution is their main goal. That takes their seemingly juvenile stunts out of the realm of wanton exhibitionism.

If this revolution talk is for real, then both sides have got the Pussy Riot story wrong. The issue is far more serious.

Judge Orders Inquest
September 24, 2012

Voice of Russia's Andrew Hiller spoke with media and business analyst William Dunkerley to learn about the case.

Q. This trial has been going on, the investigation, since at least 2006. Why has it been taking such a long time?

A. That's perhaps more a mystery then Litvinenko's death. There's been no good explanation as to why it's taking so long.

Q. What else can the British do at this point?

A. It seems to me that the entire case has been riddled with bad information and errors from the start. I find it hard to understand how a good conclusion can be reached after all this time, after having six years of no determination of the manner and cause of death. There's been no explanation as to why. Most of the news reports talk about Litvinenko being murdered by polonium but actually the coroner never ruled that his death was a homicide.

Q. Is there a lot of suspicion on the evidence or the quality of the evidence?

A. The story that has been reported in the news media has been riddled with contradictions from the start. The famous deathbed accusation that Litvinenko supposedly made against Putin is a good example of that. At first a man named Alexander Goldfarb tried to pass off the accusation as a deathbed statement dictated to him by Litvinenko. Goldfarb said he listened and took it all down, as the story goes. But then later Goldfarb confessed that the words were not those of Litvinenko's, but they were written by Goldfarb himself.

Q. How does the Litvinenko issue impact the Russia and Britain relationship? How has it moved so far?

A. It seems to have created a major fracture in the relationship between the two countries. Initially there was a mutual expulsion of diplomatic personnel, and they haven't really recovered from all that yet.

Q. Is there a rift that has not healed yet?

A. There's been some recent events that have

been more positive than the past six years. But on the other hand Cameron was very pointed to recite that the Litvinenko case remains as a sticking point between the two nations.

Q. Do you think that if this case is resolved in the courts it will lead to any resolution of the issue?

A. If it could be resolved in an honest and understandable way, but I'm not sure they're off to a very good start even with the latest hearing. Back in October, Andrew Reid, the coroner who has been working on this case since the beginning said that he was going to have an open and full investigation. He called it a fearless investigation of the full circumstances. But then he was mysteriously replaced on the case. He had called for the release of MI5 and MI6 information. And then all of a sudden he was hospitalized for appendicitis, news reports said. And then all of a sudden a scandal came up over him hiring his wife some three years ago, and he was taken off the case altogether. These seemed to be mysterious circumstances. And the new judge on the case, Sir Robert Owen, seems to be picking up from a different point from where Andrew Reid left off. Owen claims he's not going to go after the intelligence information that has been withheld. He's going to continue to withhold it, and unlike Andrew Reid, who began his statement by saying "*if* Mr. Litvinenko is shown to have died as a result of the ingestion of polonium 210," now Robert Owen seems to be beginning with the presumption that he *did* die from polonium 210. So there is a real unexplained difference in the approaches of the two people.

Judging Putin
October 16, 2012

It's time for Russian president Vladimir Putin to get serious and shape up his own image.

Fifty years ago, the Cuban Missile Crisis was the buzz-topic in America about Russia. Today, it's the Pussy Riot, a group of exhibitionists who call themselves musicians fighting oppression. In the 1960s Americans fretted over Khrushchev wanting to "bury" them. Now Americans don't consider Russia a threat to themselves; they're up in arms (figuratively) over Russia's threat to its own democracy.

What was central in the 60s isn't on the radar screen today. But, mention Khrushchev to Americans who were alive in the 60s, and you just may hear him characterized by his "we will bury you" speech.

I did a name association game with some fellow Americans. I stated the name of a former president, and asked to hear the first words that came to mind. So, "Hoover"

yielded, for instance, "Great Depression."
Roosevelt, "recovery." Nixon, "crook."

The word associations seem to encapsulate
history's judgment of those leaders. The
characterizations of the leaders represent a
narrative theme. The stories about their
presidencies are woven around it. Historians
take a deeper look. For others, it's the theme
that prevails and defines.

It's said newspapers are the first draft of
history. That's bad news for the legacy of
Vladimir Putin. The international media
mash-up on his leadership-to-date is that
he's a ruthless anti-democratic dictator who
won't go away. For the Western public, that's
the established theme. And, that's the record
that future historians will find when
researching Putin.

The most remarkable thing about this
negative theme is that it is not fact based.
Some observers imagine that a conspiracy of
world media drives the bad coverage. But
there's no real evidence of that.

The Alexander Litvinenko case exemplifies
the real process through which Putin is
regularly slimed internationally. My book,

The Phony Litvinenko Murder
(OmnicomPress.com/plm), explains this
process in detail. In a nutshell, though, this
is a case of a "managed story." The entire
news story about Putin being behind the
murder of Litvinenko was fabricated by a
non-state arch enemy of Putin's. And then it
was skillfully foisted upon an unsuspecting
press, appreciative of having an enormously
attention getting story handed to them
ready-to-use.

My study of the managed story approach
goes back to the dawn of the Putin era. I've
carefully analyzed how it has been used to
defame Russia and its leader. That gave me
the insight to see how the process can be
defeated. I know exactly how it works, what
the vulnerabilities are, and how to defeat it.

That leaves me amazed to see that Putin has
employed virtually no effective
countermeasures. It's hard to imagine why
not. Maybe it's out of ignorance of what to
do. Or perhaps it's a result of arrogance over
the need to respond at all.

The consequences are dire. Putin's failure to
protect his own image is a disservice to his
own country. It isn't just Putin's historical

legacy that's at stake. His neglect has resulted in diplomatic fractures, impeded Russia's quest to regain its place in the world, and has been a burden to international commerce and integration.

Putin's place in history is being shaped right now. The first draft of history continues to be written by enemies. His response has been to stage stunts like dressing up as a Siberian crane, and sponsoring projects to disseminate puffery. It's high time for him to get serious about protecting his own image, and to start becoming an effective steward of his country's reputation.

Russia Should Stop Shying Away From Defending Itself in the Foreign Press
October 22, 2012

Interview of William Dunkerley by noted Russian journalist Alexei Pankin.

Is it true that the West is against Russia? Is it waging a propaganda war? --Let's discuss!

If the answers to those questions are yes, how is the anti-Russian propaganda organized, and who is behind it? Is it possible to counter it? And are our authorities negligently leaving the formation the country's image to the enemies of the president? Alexei Pankin talks about all this in conversation with well-known American media analyst William Dunkerley.

Q. Bill, recently, The *Moscow Times* published a scandalous article by Steven Korn, president of the American governmentally-sponsored Radio Free Europe/Radio Liberty. In it he relates a very disparaging characterization of president Vladimir Putin. I was very struck by Mr.

Korn's sincerity. I get the feeling that he himself believes what he's written, and thinks that for English-speaking audiences all those negative allegations are self-evident. Is it true that the image of the Russian president in the West is one of a leader who is a "ruthless politician" who "dismantled Russia's democratic and free market reforms" in order to become a "totalitarian leader"?

A. Yes, that's right. According to an opinion poll in March 2012, only 15 percent of Americans have even a somewhat positive view of Putin. Over the years, the most prominent Western news stories about Russia have claimed that Putin has used energy as a weapon against Ukraine, ordered the murder of Alexander Litvinenko, and ruthlessly invaded Georgia to strangle democracy there. From the start of Putin's presidency, the news has characterized him as a sneaky former spy with an insatiable thirst for power. There was a brief reprieve from that negativity when Putin was the first foreign leader to contact the American president with sympathy over 9/11. That resulted in a surge in positive feelings toward Russia. But, there has always been a notable absence of major news stories commenting upon the improvements in Russia's economy and standard of living during Putin's tenure.

Q. You once said that it seems like Putin has been spat upon in the Western press, and all he does is wipe it off.

A. Indeed, he doesn't seem to object to the negative news stories. The trouble is that when publically-made allegations go unchallenged, they become fixed in the minds of Westerners. It's not like Putin started his Kremlin life with an established positive image. Frankly, he was an unknown in the West. So the allegations have been all that people have known of him. For most Americans, Russia is not a highly interesting news topic. The whole topic of foreign news is not of major interest here. So there is no natural curiosity to reality-test the stories Americans have heard. People just accept them. Putin's absence of response has allowed his enemies to control the story. That certainly puts him at a disadvantage in face-to-face international negotiations. Korn's article is perhaps evidence of what Putin is up against.

Recently, Putin's arch enemies have even

found success in turning negative international stories inward. That's been responsible for emboldening agitators and fomenting dissatisfaction in the heart of Russia. Putin's popularity has slipped. The negative stories are gaining ground.

It's said newspapers are the first draft of history. That's bad news for Putin. In the West he won't be judged by his achievements and failures, but by the negative allegations advanced in the media by his enemies.

Meanwhile, the Pussy Riot band of serial exhibitionists have earned themselves a so-far unchallenged place in history as recipients of the John Lennon Peace Prize for opposing Putin's purported oppression, and as the European Parliament designees as finalists for the Andrei Sakharov Prize. Western audiences would be aghast if they saw pictures of some of the young women's previous lurid exploits.

The Enemies

Q. Honestly, in Russian terms, phrases like "enemies of Russia" and "enemies of Putin" conjure up very painful recollections of the "enemies" of the Stalinist past. You are using those terms very liberally.

A. I wouldn't agree that I use the terms liberally. Modern warfare includes cyber attacks and advanced psychological warfare. The definition of an enemy can no longer be limited to foreign countries. After 9/11, the United States became acutely aware of what it is like to have non-state enemies. I think that Putin needs to awake to the realities that he faces. He seems to want to conceive of things primarily in state-against-state terms. It may also be repulsive to him to believe that he and the Russian state may have mortal enemies that were born and raised on Russian soil. Russia and Putin himself would be better served if he reacted to the real situation.

Although, I don't know the totality of the threat Putin faces, I have carefully studied what happened in the Litvinenko case. It clearly represented a media-based attack against Putin. And there, the finger of suspicion points to persons who were born in Russia, but are now closely connected with London.

Q. And so we pick up on the story of Russia's "non-state" enemies...

A. Let's discuss this by concrete example. The Alexander Litvinenko case illustrates the process through which Putin is regularly slimed internationally. My book, *The Phony Litvinenko Murder*, explains this process in detail. In a nutshell, though, this is a case of a "managed story." The entire Western news story about Putin being behind the murder of Litvinenko was fabricated apparently by the Berezovsky camp. And then it was skillfully foisted upon unsuspecting Western media who were appreciative of getting an enormously attention getting story handed to them ready-to-use.

The story told is specious, but believable by the uninformed. The famous deathbed statement is a good example. That's the statement where Litvinenko accused Putin as being behind the poisoning. At first, an associate of Berezovsky's said it was dictated to him by Litvinenko just before his death. The associate said he wrote down Litvinenko's words. Later he confessed they weren't Litvinenko's words at all. Litvinenko didn't dictate anything. It was written by that associate. I didn't see where any journalists called attention to that discrepancy. But when facts change to suit the convenience of the news source, it reflects on the credibility of the whole story. Another issue is that news reports called Litvinenko a former spy. But there's no indication that he ever did espionage work. Even his wife has explained that he never was a spy.

Q. In September, the London Coroner resumed investigating the case after a six-year hiatus. One independent London-based analyst suggested in a *KP* interview that the coroner may claim to be trying to establish the truth, but the prosecutor and the press will continue to spew the Berezovsky version. In any event, this seems destined to impact Russia's reputation negatively.

A. I would be very surprised if the coroner arrives at an honest verdict. The inquest procedure has telltale signs of being rigged. There has been no explanation why after almost six years there has not been even a conclusion on whether or not Litvinenko's death was a homicide. When Coroner Andrew Reid reopened activity on the case, he called for disclosure of MI5/MI6 documents that are relevant. But then it was reported that Reid was suddenly stricken by appendicitis and hospitalized. Next a scandal erupted over Reid's employment of his wife several years earlier, and he was removed from the case. A new coroner was then appointed, who announced that the secret documents would not be disclosed.

Meanwhile, I've also seen collusive-sounding intersections between the prosecutor who formulated Britain's allegations of Russian state involvement in Litvinenko's death, and people connected to Boris Berezovsky. A lot of other inconsistencies in the case exist, as well. There seems to be a keen attempt to avoid full disclosure. Even if the coroner were to arrive at a verdict soon, there is every reason to distrust it.

Coroner Reid himself stated that "public interest plainly demands an open and fearless investigation into the full circumstances." He went on to say, "any lesser level of inquiry would not command public confidence either nationally or internationally." But now it seems that the public will indeed get a lesser level of inquiry. Relevant documents will be withheld.

Reid is wrong about public confidence, though. Western audiences won't distrust rigged results. That's because all they're likely to see is continuation of the mythological version of the case, the "managed story" put forward by Putin's enemies.

In my opinion, the whole case should simply be dismissed. There is little chance for a legitimate outcome. Not only is there reason to distrust whatever verdict may arise, but hasn't the basis for going forward vanished? Coroner Reid ruled that "the whole purpose of the inquest is to investigate the credibility of the competing theories." That would mean: no competing theory, no problem. In the Berezovsky v. Abramovich case, the High Court judge ruled that Berezovsky is "inherently unreliable." That would mean that his theory in the Litvinenko case can not be relied upon. If one discounts Berezovsky's theory that Putin is behind Litvinenko's death, doesn't that mean there are no competing theories to investigate? Why are the British going to spend a reported $6 million on a seemingly pointless inquest? Doesn't it seem like there must be an ulterior motive?

Vigorous Resistance

Q. Okay, let's consider that the campaigns against the Russian president did not erupt spontaneously, and that they were skillfully directed. In that case, it is easy to speculate that the upcoming Olympic Games in Sochi will be an opportunity for new attacks. I remember that on the eve of the St. Petersburg G8 summit in 2006, there was talk of excluding Russia from this elite club. The 2014 Olympics are widely regarded as a personal project of Putin's. The event is very important for all Russians. Are these festivities destined to be spoiled? Or can trouble be preempted?

A. There is good reason to suspect that media-based attacks against Putin are opportunistic. Politkovskaya was killed on Putin's birthday. The media blitz over Litvinenko occurred while Putin was attending the Asia Pacific Economic Cooperation Summit in Hanoi. The Sochi Olympics present Putin's enemies with an obvious opportunity.

Of course, it is possible to employ preemptive tactics. But victory will not be simple, and there is scant time left to do an effective job.

I've studied the media-based attacks since the dawn of the Putin era. I've carefully analyzed how they have been used to defame Russia and its leader. That gave me the insight to see how the process can be defeated. I know exactly how it works, what the vulnerabilities are, and how to defeat it.

That leaves me amazed to see that Putin has employed virtually no effective countermeasures since day one of his rule. It's hard to imagine why not. Maybe it's out of ignorance of what to do. Or perhaps it's a result of arrogance over the need to respond at all.

What can preempt an unfortunate scenario at the Olympics? I say that the first step must be an attitude change on the part of Putin. Isn't it high time for him to get serious about protecting his own image, and to start becoming an effective steward of his country's reputation? This is not a private matter, but a matter of national importance.

Startling New Twist in Litvinenko Death Case
November 12, 2012

A step forward toward openness? Or just a sham gesture?

The British inquiry into the 2006 death of Alexander Litvinenko has taken a dramatic turn in direction. Just two months ago the London Coroner appeared focused on investigating alleged Russian state involvement in the death, and on steadfastly upholding MI5/MI6 secrecy about the case.

But a November 2 hearing conducted by coroner Sir Robert Owen has thrown things wide open. Earlier he seemed intent only on following a trail back to Moscow. Now, he's apparently changed his mind. Multiple additional theories of culpability have been put on the table, including that of the British state.

The Litvinenko affair has been a high-profile international murder mystery ever since the subject's death by poisoning in London. Accusations that Russian president Vladimir Putin was behind it fueled intense media attention. The general storyline is that Litvinenko was a former spy murdered by radioactive polonium on orders of Putin, who allegedly wanted him silenced.

Careful independent analysis, however, has shown that the mainstream media narrative of the case was fabricated and has no factual basis. It's never been officially determined that Litvinenko was even murdered. And, there's no reliable evidence that he was ever a spy. The media accounts on those issues are specious.

It has been reported that the manufactured story was spread by people connected to Boris Berezovsky. They apparently concocted the tale of espionage, revenge, and murder, and fed it to unsuspecting media outlets hungry for a juicy story. I've documented all this in my book, *The Phony Litvinenko Murder* (www.omnicompress.com/plm).

Berezovsky is a wealthy arch-enemy of Putin's who resides in London, hiding from criminal convictions back in Russia. He is an erstwhile Putin ally turned outspoken critic. Berezovsky is reported to be organizing a revolution to overthrow Putin by force and replace the constitution.

Perhaps it should be no surprise that the London Coroner has done a turnabout in the death inquiry. The Litvinenko case has been full of unexpected twists and turns. At first, Litvinenko said he believed an Italian named Mario Scaramella had poisoned him. Then after Litvinenko died, a well publicized deathbed statement appeared accusing Putin. Alexander Goldfarb, an associate of Berezovsky's, claimed Litvinenko dictated it to him on his deathbed. Later, Goldfarb confessed it was he who wrote the words, not Litvinenko.

In 2011, then Coroner Andrew Reid had ruled that "the whole purpose of the inquest is to investigate the credibility of the competing theories." But the only theory given prominence was Berezovsky's contention that Putin was behind the alleged murder. In an August 2012 civil decision involving Berezovsky, the High Court judge ruled that Berezovsky is 'inherently unreliable.' Wouldn't that mean that his theory in the Litvinenko case could not be relied upon?

That left things looking like there was really no reason for the inquest. If there were no competing theories to investigate, why were the British going to spend a reported $6 million on a seemingly pointless inquest? Was there an ulterior motive?

Now that the inquiry is wide open, what could explain the marked change in direction? The previous hearing held on September 20 seemingly affirmed a demand for a "criminal investigation of the Russian state." No other specific targets of investigation were mentioned.

At the November hearing, however, a long list of possible targets suddenly appeared. It includes: Mario Scaramella, Boris Berezovsky, the Spanish Mafia, Chechen-related groups, and the British state itself. The coroner will also consider whether suicide or an accident might be involved. What a change from just suspecting Putin!

Even the transcript of that hearing, however, provided no clues as to why the hyper focus on Russia was dropped.

One possible intervening event did occur between the September and November hearings. An October article in *Komsomolskaya Pravda*, Russia's largest newspaper, accused the coroner's inquiry of appearing rigged against Russia.

In the article, Alexei Pankin, one of the country's most distinguished journalists, interviewed me on the results of my research. I explained how the original coroner on the case, Andrew Reid, had been suspiciously removed from the proceedings. I also described collusive-appearing intersections between the prosecutor, who formulated Britain's allegations of Russian state involvement, and people connected to Berezovsky.

There had been no explanation of why after six years there hadn't been a conclusion on whether or not Litvinenko's death was a homicide, I pointed out, adding, "I would be very surprised if the coroner arrives at an honest verdict. The inquest procedure has telltale signs of being rigged."

That *Komsomolskaya Pravda* interview was also picked up internationally by several prominent English language news outlets.

Less than two weeks later, Coroner Owen surprisingly threw open the scope of the inquiry. Suddenly there is a multitude of competing theories ripe for investigation, not just Berezovsky's. The exclusively Russian focus is gone. Owen understandably may not want to follow in Reid's footsteps.

It's curious that Reid had focused on such a narrow scope. At his October 2011 hearing he seemed to proclaim a mandate to investigate "the alleged criminal role of the Russian state." But the charter of the coroner's office specifically forbids it from determining criminal liability.

It is clear that the Berezovsky camp is pushing for the coroner to pursue the Russian state. The widow Litvinenko, who is closely associated with Berezovsky, urged Coroner Owen to endorse Reid's position. But Owen demurred, saying "the scope is a matter that I have continually to review in the light of the information and material that I see." Perhaps Reid had been bamboozled into undertaking an investigation that was not his business. Good for Owen for getting straight on that one.

Prosecutorial Indiscretion in Litvinenko Case
December 11, 2012

Suspicion, suspicion, suspicion. Is no one paying attention?

Suspicious connections in the Alexander Litvinenko death case prosecution have received little media attention. They reach deep into British official circles. Litvinenko was a reputed former Russian spy who died mysteriously in London in 2006. News reports claimed he was murdered with radioactive polonium on orders of Russian president Vladimir Putin.

But a careful analysis now shows a murky web of affiliations and intersections that call into question the whole media story. It also casts serious suspicion upon the integrity of the British investigation and prosecution.

Here's what analysis shows: There are connections between the man who was the British Crown Prosecutor at the time of Litvinenko's death, and the attorney who has been representing the widow Litvinenko, and with the attorney representing the

Russian accused by the prosecutor of murder.

Curiously, when prosecutor Ken MacDonald had announced intentions to charge that Russian, Andrew Lugovoi, with the murder of Litvinenko, the London corner had never concluded that Litvinenko was indeed murdered. MacDonald's action was widely regarded as affirming the allegation that Vladimir Putin was somehow behind Litvinenko's death. That accusation was made by Boris Berezovsky, a wealthy arch-enemy of Putin's who resides in London, hiding from criminal convictions back in Russia. MacDonald's siding with Berezovsky led to the serious and yet unresolved rift between the United Kingdom and Russia.

But MacDonald's history and connections are enough to raise suspicions. He served as head of the Crown Prosecution Service from 2003 to 2008. He came to that office from Matrix Chambers, a law firm he helped found in 2000. Following his government service, he returned to his law firm in 2008.

Ben Emerson is an attorney representing widow Marina Litvinenko. He too is employed at Matrix Chambers, and with

MacDonald, was one of its founders.

The man MacDonald accused of murdering Litvinenko, Andrei Lugovoi, is reportedly represented by Jessica Simor, an attorney also at Matrix chambers. Media reports say she works at Matrix with Cherie Booth, another founder of the firm. At the time when MacDonald's charges caused the rift between the UK and Russia, Booth's husband, Tony Blair, was prime minister of the UK. Before leaving the government, MacDonald was knighted for his service, and now enjoys the title "Lord Ken MacDonald."

I'm not sure what all that adds up to, but I do believe that it should be disclosed.

Clearly, the media that has covered the Litvinenko case has neglected to focus attention on this suspicious web of interconnections. What's more, former prosecutor MacDonald seems to have been less than transparent himself. Just last year the *New York Times* quoted him as saying he has the "gravest suspicions" of Moscow's involvement in the Litvinenko case. But the report doesn't mention all his entanglements with players on various sides of this mystery.

In the Litvinenko case, Matrix Chambers appears to be not a "matrix" at all, but instead a "locus" of activity.

This week there will be another pre-inquest hearing on the Litvinenko death. There was a dramatic turn of events at the previous hearing. Originally, focus had been on the Berezovsky implication of Putin. But suddenly a new coroner, Sir Robert Owen, has thrown things wide open. Now even British culpability in the death is said to be considered. Some say that move is just a ruse in response to accusations that the inquest is rigged in favor of Berezovsky's version. The results of the hearing may shed light on that.

In the meantime, the widow Litvinenko has plaintively implored, "It's important we know the truth." She's previously revealed a belief that her husband was the victim of a Kremlin plot. Now she hopes the inquest will "discredit competing theories." That doesn't sound like an open quest for the truth to me. But she's requesting financial donations to support that quest. She says that Berezovsky has stopped paying Matrix Chambers for work on the case because he is now broke. Her plea for money, however, has been spectacularly publicized, and smacks of the

Berezovsky PR machine still at work.

Moscow Times Files False Report on Litvinenko Hearing
December 17, 2012

First a false report. Then a report on a hearing that never happened.

"Russia Implicated in Litvinenko Death," The *Moscow Times*, December 14, 2012 appears to tell what happened at a London hearing on the suspicious death of Alexander Litvinenko. Unfortunately it paints a false picture.

The story claims the hearing was told that "an initial assessment of evidence showed that the Russian state is to blame for the mysterious poisoning of the Kremlin dissident."

But it wasn't told that.

Instead, the record reflects that Hugh Davies, lead lawyer for the inquest, presented his review of government material assembled on the 2006 case. What Davies *actually* said was that on *first impression* this specific material reflects a culpability of the Russian state.

But that's not all Davies said. He qualified that comment by adding that this conclusion was reached by taking the government material in *isolation*. In other words, the conclusion excludes consideration of other material such as publicly available information or material that has been disclosed by other interested parties. He emphasized that the conclusion relates "solely to the effect of the government material taken alone."

In my research, I've found reason to question the integrity of the government's case. There are suspicious connections between the man who was the British Crown Prosecutor at the time of Litvinenko's death, and the attorney who has been representing the widow Litvinenko, and with the attorney representing the Russian accused by the prosecutor of murder. There is also involvement of the wife of Tony Blair who was the UK prime minister at the time.

Davies didn't tell the hearing that the Russian state is to blame. In fact, he was quick to clarify that the Coroner's court "has made no factual findings whatsoever so far." What he did acknowledge is simply that on the face of things, the government has material that supports the claim of Russian state culpability. He made clear that is not necessarily the whole story. Separately, Davies went beyond surface appearances of the government's case and did his own detailed assessment. But it was redacted from the record.

The *Moscow Times* took another wrong step when it quoted Mark Galeotti who it called an expert on Russian crime and a researcher at New York University. According to Galeotti, "the discovery of polonium already is very strong evidence of state involvement because only sophisticated nuclear laboratories can produce the rare element in necessary quantities." Polonium is rumored to have been the agent of poisoning in the Litvinenko case.

But Galeotti's notion was contradicted by testimony at the hearing. Neil Garnham, lawyer for the British Home Office spoke to the polonium issue, saying, "the more likely source of the polonium, and this is a submission I make, is from an industrial or commercial application, not from a power station or nuclear weapons programme." Also, terrorism and Russia expert Gordon Hahn has noted that "polonium is readily available on the illegal black market."

In all, the depiction of the hearing given in the *Moscow Times* significantly deviates from the facts, and leaves readers with a very mistaken impression. I don't know whether or not the Russian state was involved in Litvinenko's death. But playing loose with the facts detracts from a real quest for the truth.

One final goof. In the *Moscow Times* article, author Nikolas von Twickel claimed that the hearing would be continuing on the following day, Friday, December 14. But that too was not factual. At the close of the Thursday session it was clearly announced there would not be a continuation. The hearing ended, as indicated, on Thursday.

Putin's Opposition Scores Big at Critical London Hearing
December 20, 2012

Putin seems to be losing this battle.

The facts said one thing. The media told a different story. And Russian president Vladimir Putin lost another skirmish with his enemies in the process.

This drama unfolded in the London Coroner's court on December 13. The 2006 death of reputed former spy Alexander Litvinenko was the subject. When the hearing was over, media headlines cried out:

--Russia Implicated in Litvinenko Death (The *Moscow Times*)
--British evidence 'shows Russia involved' (The *Guardian*)
--Russian state involved in ex-KGB agent Litvinenko's death (CNN)

The *Moscow Times* even elaborated on the theme. It claimed the hearing was told that "an initial assessment of evidence showed that the Russian state is to blame for the mysterious poisoning of the Kremlin dissident."

The only problem is that's not what really was said. The media outlets filed false reports.

Specious media accounts are not new in the Litvinenko case. Putin was accused of being behind the suspicious death. But virtually the entire story surrounding that allegation is based on fabrications not facts. A wealthy arch-enemy of Putin's, Boris Berezovsky, seems to have been the mastermind behind it. His publicly-stated agenda is to bring about a violent revolution in Russia. The first shots of that revolution have been ringing out in the form of malevolent media attacks like this one.

What really did happen at the London hearing? The lead lawyer in the inquest, Hugh Davies, presented a very technical analysis of the government's case that alleges Russian state involvement. He reported that the government's material gives a first impression that the Russian state is culpable. But he said that impression arises "solely to the effect of the government material taken alone." It doesn't take into account, for example, "material that is publicly available or material that has been disclosed by other interested persons." In other words, it's not the whole story.

But that didn't stop the media outlets from reporting otherwise. They made it sound like the blame had conclusively been pinned on the Kremlin. Davies even clarified that the Coroner's court "has made no factual findings whatsoever so far."

Certainly none of this exculpates Putin or the Russian state. But it's far short of being conclusive about their involvement. An honest inquiry into the facts and a look at the whole picture would be needed to sort things out.

In my own research I've actually found reason to question the integrity of the government's case. There are suspicious connections between the man who was the British Crown Prosecutor at the time of Litvinenko's death, and the attorney who has been representing the widow Litvinenko, and with the attorney representing the Russian accused by the prosecutor of murder. There is also involvement of the wife of Tony Blair who was the UK prime minister at the time. Interestingly, the case resulted in a major fracture in relations between Britain and Russia.

How did the media get their reports on the hearing so wrong? I haven't investigated the mechanism in this instance. But I did look into how the explosive story about Putin's involvement got started six years ago. I wrote a book about it called *The Phony Litvinenko Murder*. In it I detail how Berezovsky appears to have engaged a high power PR agency to put out the bogus story. Media outlets were given photos and press releases, offered explanations and interviews, and ended up with a highly captivating story to titillate their audiences. Unfortunately there was no due diligence by the media to debunk the specious allegations. That seems to be the case today, as well.

There are a host of contradictions and unexplained circumstances that any inquisitive journalist covering this story should have looked into. Here are a few:

--The government's case accuses Russian Andrei Lugovoi of murdering Litvinenko. Yet the hearing spoke of Russian state culpability. At the time of Litvinenko's death there was no known or alleged existing connection between Lugovoi and the Russian government. How did the focus move from Lugovoi to the Russian state?

--Davies alleged that at first glance the government's material holds evidence of Kremlin involvement. Yet just last year the prosecutor who had collected that so-called evidence told the *New York Times* that he had the "gravest suspicions of Moscow involvement." There is a world of difference between a grave suspicion and hard evidence. Is there an explanation for this astonishing disparity?

--One preoccupation at the December 13 hearing was whether the British state neglected to protect Litvinenko from known danger. But the job of the coroner is to determine the manner and cause of death. Why is the subject of negligence coming before him? Some say all the rhetoric about state negligence is laying the groundwork for a law suit for damages. Presumably British taxpayers would foot the bill. Is the coroner being manipulated to serve someone's private purposes?

The rules that govern the coroner's work

forbid him from venturing outside the responsibility of finding the manner and cause of death. The charter of his office specifically forbids him from determining criminal liability. There is one narrow exception. He can stray from his main purpose only if it is to allay public fears.

The coroner now appears engaged in a wide ranging search that smacks of looking for criminal culpability. Perhaps it's being done to soothe public fears. But consider where any such fears may have come from.

A lawyer reportedly being paid by Berezovsky has been widely quoted using the phrase "state-sponsored nuclear terrorism on the streets of London" in regard to the Litvinenko case. There's been other highly-charged rhetoric, too. If there are public fears, were they inspired by Berezovsky's media campaign?

Did he create the pretext for the coroner to use a highly-conspicuous hearing to delve into matters that otherwise would be off limits? Berezovsky's civil war aspirations are clearly advanced by all the focus on possible Russian state involvement in Litvinenko's death. Is the coroner aiding and abetting insurrectionists?

Another major focus of the hearing was arguments on Berezovsky's behalf that the inquest should be prevented from considering Berezovsky's own possible involvement in Litvinenko's death. The incessant assertions conjure up the famous Shakespeare quotation, "The lady doth protest too much, methinks." Why is avoiding scrutiny so important to Berezovsky?

These certainly sound like juicy tidbits worthy of journalistic investigation by media outlets. But instead of digging into them, the media just picked up another phony story and ran with it.

It's Time for Putin and Obama to Have an Urgent Talk
December 28, 2012

Manipulation and misunderstanding rule the day.

American legislators passed the Magnitsky bill to punish Russia for "human rights violations." In retaliation, Russian legislators enacted the Dima Yakovlev bill as punishment to America. President Obama has signed his bill into law. As of this writing, president Putin has not yet followed suit. Does he really have to join in this foolish game and open the door to another round?

I've seen Putin handle apparent humiliation with great magnanimity before. But he's failed to draw upon those skills now.

For himself, Obama must deal with many members of Congress who, believe me, do not realize that they are being manipulated. So now Obama has signed into law a bill that is based on false premises. And that leaves the Russian president to decide whether to respond in kind to this provocation.

What can the president do in such a situation? I think Putin would only benefit if people here could come to understand what he is dealing with. Few Americans know that Russia has non-state enemies who maliciously seek to destabilize the country and undermine the constitution. It would be wise if Putin would explain all that to Obama as soon as possible. And then he should explain to Americans directly that their government is making matters worse for everyone by its misguided attempts to influence Russia's domestic affairs.

Putin Bans Orphan Adoption by Americans
December 28, 2012

What a limp way to fight and fight back.

Are American and Russian legislators competing to see who is the most foolish? It seems so. First the Americans passed the Magnitsky bill to punish Russia for alleged human-rights abuses. Then the Russians enacted the Dima Yakovlev bill as retaliative punishment for the Americans.

President Obama has signed the American bill into law. And now President Putin has signed the bill handed to him. It is lamentable that they have joined in this foolish game. Won't their actions only lead to further tit-for-tat responses?

Putin has called the Magnitsky bill an unacceptable humiliation. But I've seen him handle apparent humiliation with greater magnanimity before.

I was in the audience when in 2006 president Putin addressed the World Newspaper Congress in the State Kremlin

Palace in Moscow. Three National Bolsheviks penetrated security and started shouting their rallying cry, "Russia without Putin," while throwing leaflets into the air.

Another national leader might have felt humiliated by this happening in front of leading journalists from around the world. But Putin handled it with aplomb. He explained to his audience that the hall they were in had been built by the Communists to host party congresses. "It's true," Putin glibly remarked, that "Bolsheviks still come to this hall, but now in a different capacity." The audience chuckled. Putin looked the statesman, the Bolsheviks the fools.

That's the Putin who could have more constructively resolved this ridiculous situation created by the legislators.

President Obama, before signing the Magnitsky bill, had never been in favor of it. He publically stated that it is unnecessary. Indeed, it is not even an American initiative. My research has found it was sponsored by international provocateurs who apparently seek to destabilize the Russian state and delegitimize its leaders.

It is perplexing why Obama signed the Magnitsky bill. But he is faced with a legislature that has been successfully duped by Russia's enemies into believing the issue has legitimacy. This isn't the first time they were duped. There have been other specious anti-Russian assaults perpetrated through the media. They were chronicled in headlines such as "Russia invades Georgia," and "Kremlin murders journalists." Thanks to the media, much of the American public believes these stories, too.

The provocateurs make skillful use of lobbying and media-spin techniques. A group of Russian and American experts have formulated a plan called "Russia without Spin" (www.russiawithoutspin.com) to serve as a countermeasure. But so far the Kremlin has not been receptive to it.

So Obama has signed into law a bill that is based on false premises. And now Putin has signed the Dima Yakovlev bill in response. In doing so, Putin ironically validated the villainous picture his enemies have painted of him. Unwittingly he played right into their hands.

The timing on both sides couldn't be worse.

The American bill vilifies Russia for internal problems it is already trying to fix. The Russian bill, curtailing American adoption of Russian children, comes in the aftermath of the recent mass murder of 20 children in the Newtown, located in my home state of Connecticut. That seems in extremely poor taste. The *Nation* magazine editor Katrina vanden Heuvel has called it a "major strategic mistake."

But what can the two presidents do now? How can they avoid further escalation? They should start a dialogue. There is not much understanding in the United States that Russia has non-state enemies who seek to destabilize the country and undermine the constitution. Perhaps Putin is too proud to talk much about that. But he is being judged harshly in the world, and his image would be aided if people knew and understood the problems he faces. Putin would benefit by explaining all that to Obama. And then he should explain to Americans directly that their government is making matters worse for everyone by its misguided attempts to influence Russia's domestic affairs.

Vladimir Putin's PR Blunders Earn Him Controversial Nomination
January 17, 2013

Is self hatred afoot, or is it inattention to duty?

During the tenure of Vladimir Putin, the international reputation of Russia and its leaders has been severely tarnished by his foreign and domestic critics. My research has shown that much of the criticism lacks a factual basis. But the allegations have become widely accepted, I have found, because Putin failed to protect his image and that of the country. For that reason, I've nominated him for membership in the Fanny Kaplan Club of the American University in Moscow.

When inaugurating the Fanny Kaplan Club last year, Dr. Edward Lozansky, president of the American University in Moscow, said, "To qualify you must be known as one of the most outspoken Putin haters."

It may seem strange that I've nominated

Putin to a club that exists to recognize Putin haters. But, it appears to me that Putin has done more than any other person to engender Putin hatred. Not by his actions. Mostly by his inaction. His absence of any effective response to the persistent denigration of Russia and its leaders has done more to solidify the near-universal negative images that prevail than the work of any other individual.

The problem is that for too long Putin has allowed his enemies to define him. They've been in control of his image. Over the years allegations have been successfully advanced that he blew up apartment buildings in Russia, used energy as a weapon against other countries, practiced pedophilia, murdered journalists, poisoned Alexander Litvinenko, invaded Georgia, and the list goes on. In each case the allegations have lacked a factual basis. They were fabricated.

In the Litvinenko matter, I've shown in my book, the *The Phony Litvinenko Murder*, how the media story that blamed Putin was fabricated by his arch enemies. On the Georgian invasion, the European Union's fact-finding mission reported that instead of Russia invading Georgia, the 2008 conflict started with a massive Georgian artillery attack.

Despite such factual revelations, the malicious stories propagated by Putin's enemies remain the mainstream understanding of those situations. Putin has taken no effective action to redefine perceptions along more factual lines.

What's worse, his more recent actions have strongly reinforced that negative imagery. I'm talking about the way he handled media aspects of the crackdown on NGOs in Russia; the prosecution of a so-called punk-rock protest group; and the buffoonish ban on American adoptions of Russian orphans. The result is that Putin is being held prisoner within the villainous image his enemies have created.

It was one thing when he was just a victim of media attacks advanced by others. But it's a different story now that he's foolishly playing into the hands of his enemies. The present situation strongly compels action by those concerned for Russian-American relations. His nomination to the Fanny Kaplan Club is one step in that direction.

By not acting decisively and effectively to the onslaught of negative attacks in the media, Putin is neglecting his responsibility to protect the image of his country. All the negative media coverage isn't doing much good for Russia's position in the world and relations with the United States.

Putin seems oblivious to his own pernicious role in all of this. And apparently no one around him is willing to confront him with his own failing. So, he is left like a guy with bad breath surrounded by friends unwilling to tell him. When it comes to media relations, Putin has bad breath. Someone must tell him before he offends the world further.

Some observers believe that there is nothing Putin can do to stop the malicious propaganda war being waged against him. That may be true. However, it is not predestined how people will interpret and react to those fabricated incriminations. The key isn't how he is portrayed, but how those portrayals are interpreted. I can see vast unexploited opportunities therein.

Putin's and Russia's negative international images do not represent an intractable problem. They are a result of negative media spin that has been nurtured by Putin's enemies. There is a Russian-American private sector countermeasures initiative that I strongly support. It is called "Russia without Spin" (www.russiawithoutspin.com). It stands out as a promising solution on the horizon.

(P.S. The nomination of Putin for membership in the Fanny Kaplan Club was ultimately unsuccessful.)

British Litvinenko Case against Russia Disintegrating
March 6, 2013

What a swamp this has become.

The British case against the Russian state in the Alexander Litvinenko matter seems to be teetering on the verge of collapse. Litvinenko is a reputed former Russian spy who died in London in 2006 suspiciously of poisoning. The London Coroner has been unable to reach a conclusion on whether the death was a homicide. Nevertheless for years the government has been pursuing a legal case that contends Litvinenko was murdered at the behest of the Russian government.

The London Coroner's court held pre-inquest hearings on February 27 and 28. The coroner claims to be trying to find out what really happened to Litvinenko. But the recent hearings didn't seem to clear the air on any key issue.

All along, the basis of the government's case has seemed to be nothing more than specious allegations of Boris Berezovsky and his associates. Berezovsky is a fugitive

Russian billionaire hiding out in London. Now new actions by his team are further muddling the British proceedings. They are contending that Russia and Britain are conspiring to suppress potentially relevant secret British documents.

That alleged collusion, however, looks like a hoax. I could find no record of any statement from a Russian official supporting the claim or advocating for a lack of transparency. The news reports are filled with the contentions of the Berezovsky people. What they are saying appears to be sheer fabrication. But world news outlets have fallen for the phony story hook, line, and sinker.

The Berezovsky team has been long involved in advancing scurrilous allegations against Russia and its president through the media. They've painted quite a dismal picture, albeit one not based on facts. Now it looks like they have made a pawn of the British legal system in the Litvinenko case to further their aims.

The Russian-British-collusion claim arose on February 25, when the *Guardian* reported that British media groups joined together in a legal challenge. They are fighting attempts by British foreign secretary William Hague to conceal sensitive documents. Hague contends that disclosure could harm the British public and national interests.

Guardian journalist Luke Harding relied on statements from Berezovsky associate Alexander Goldfarb who took issue with Hague's rationale. Goldfarb asserted, "[Hague's] afraid Putin will not vote the way he wants in the UN or squeeze Britain's interests." But Goldfarb didn't say where he obtained that information.

Goldfarb is the guy who claimed in 2006 that Litvinenko dictated to him a deathbed allegation that Putin was behind his poisoning. That turned out to be a hoax, too. Goldfarb later confessed that the so-called deathbed statement contained his words, not Litvinenko's. It is puzzling why Harding would rely upon such a questionable source.

Lawyer Ben Emmerson also chimed in. He's widely reported to have been paid by Berezovsky to represent the widow Litvinenko. Emmerson joined Goldfarb in accusing British leaders of being in cahoots with the Kremlin. He called it a cover-up to avoid antagonizing President Vladimir Putin. Emmerson said the British are "dancing to the Russian tarantella."

It is interesting that Emmerson should talk of the appearance of collusion. Ken MacDonald, the prosecutor who alleged Russian state involvement in Litvinenko's death in 2006, was a founding partner with Emmerson at the law firm where the two still work. MacDonald had taken leave from the firm from 2003 to 2008 to become Britain's chief prosecutor. He oversaw the formulation of the prosecution's position in the Litvinenko case.

It was during MacDonald's tenure that Berezovsky leveled his allegations against Putin. A British newspaper headline, referencing Berezovsky, cried out, "Putin tried to kill my friend, claims Russian billionaire." Berezovsky offered no facts to substantiate his claim. And likewise the British prosecution service hasn't shown much evidence beyond Berezovsky's allegation.

In October 2011, MacDonald, by then the former prosecutor, told the *New York Times* that he has the "gravest suspicions" of Moscow's involvement in the Litvinenko case. Surely grave suspicions do not constitute evidence under British law. But it looks like the British case doesn't really amount to anything more than Berezovsky's unsupported claims and a British prosecutor's hunch that the allegations are true.

But why would the Berezovsky camp want to foist upon the public that fake claim of Russian-British collusion to suppress relevant secret documents? There's some speculation that accusing the British of conspiring with Russia is just an attempt to pressure authorities to release the information. The Berezovsky team has been pushing hard for the release. It's unclear why this is such a big issue for them. Presumably they don't know what's in the documents and whether they would help or hurt in advancing their accusations against Putin.

Meanwhile, Mrs. Litvinenko clamors for justice for her long-deceased husband. But what about justice for Andrei Lugovoi and Dmitry Kovtun? They are two Russian citizens who live under the suspicion of murder charges based on MacDonald's case. How will they ever receive justice in Britain? The charges appear to have stemmed from fraudulent allegations and mere grave suspicions.

So it seems that the entire Litvinenko murder saga reported in the press was originally touched off by statements of Berezovsky's. Were they reliable? The answer came last year during a high-stakes civil trial in London involving Berezovsky. The presiding judge issued an official finding: Berezovsky is "inherently unreliable."

That means the whole prosecution case seems based upon the rantings of a person who can't be trusted. With all the current and past shenanigans in London over the Litvinenko case, who is going to consider whatever verdict might be returned to be credible? That's why the case teeters on the verge of collapse.

The media group's request for full disclosure will be given further consideration by the court. Some of the secret information may get released.

But, I think they should stop squabbling about whether or not to release it and just close the case. It has been bungled beyond the point of believability.

British Litvinenko Death Inquest Descends into Farce
March 18, 2013

Inquest spirals out of control.

The main question arising from last Thursday's hearing in the British Litvinenko death case is whether anyone is actually in charge of the proceedings. Media reports quickly focused on the announced postponement of the May 1 final inquest. Now it's been put off until October.

But the reasons for the delay tell the bigger story: coroner Sir Robert Owen seems to have lost control of the proceedings, if he ever really had it. The inquest's own legal counsel recited a litany of examples:

--The British government ignored for 10 long months the coroner's request for relevant documents.
--A request for telephone evidence from the Metropolitan Police has not yet been completed.
--Scientific evidence from the police won't be available until the end of April.
--Statements from known witnesses won't be

available until the end of April or later.

Keep in mind that we're talking about a death that occurred in 2006. Not ready yet? Who's going to believe that story?

What's more, although the hearing was called to hear applications from parties wishing to give testimony anonymously, none were heard. They weren't ready.

Perhaps as a reflection of his impotence in the case, Owen lashed out with an order of press censorship. He threatens contempt of court charges against journalists and media organizations that publish anything that so much as tends to identify anonymous witnesses. Tends to identify? In whose view? Owen's, I guess. It is completely subjective, and puts Owen in a clear position to intimidate the British press.

The most recent hearing wasn't the first time that Owen's lack of control has been apparent. At the February 27th hearing, he lost control to parties associated with Boris Berezovsky. About half of that hearing was controlled by those people as they advanced the ridiculous accusation that Russia and Britain were conspiring to withhold information vital to the case. If Owen had any control, he should have shut down that nonsense right away.

The Berezovsky clan offered no substantiation for its claims. The contentions turned out to be pure fabrication, just like Berezovsky's initial allegation that President Vladimir Putin ordered Litvinenko's poisoning. Frankly, I don't know whether Putin did or didn't. But Berezovsky and his companions have certainly offered no factual basis for their claims. And they have a long record of inventing false stories to put Putin in a bad light.

If British governmental departments can ignore Owen with impunity, perhaps Prime Minister David Cameron should personally take charge. Presumably he'd be able to enforce compliance. But I don't think even that would bring this case to a believable conclusion. The record has become confounded by lies and fabricated stories. They've apparently permeated the official case. There is little chance of ever finding the truth. The honest course would be to admit that the truth is unattainable, and just dismiss the case and avoid further national embarrassment.

Another "Murder" or Just Grave Suspicions Instead of Evidence Again
March 27, 2013

Berezovsky found dead!

Despite the fact that British authorities have dispelled claims that Boris Berezovsky was murdered by strangulation or that he died by natural causes, many news outlets have been running stories advancing conspiracy theories, hinting at "murder." Most quote people associated with Berezovsky as sources. A lot of these people previously supported Berezovsky's allegations that the Russian state, and Russia's president Vladimir Putin in particular, were behind the 2006 death in London of Alexander Litvinenko, the controversial consultant to several intelligence services.

An *Irish Independent* headline read, "No suicide, says Litvinenko's wife." The *Guardian* quoted Nikolai Glushkov, a person identified as a friend of Berezovsky: "I'm definite Boris was killed. I have quite different information from what is being published in the media." After hearing an account from Berezovsky's ex-wife Galina, he remarked "A scarf was there. There were traces of him being strangled around the neck."

In Russia, overzealous anti-Berezovsky conspiracy theorists are adding their part to the confusion. The *Mail* reported that former politician Sergei Markov said "the tycoon was assassinated because he knew too much about Western plots to undermine Putin and planned to trade this knowledge for a return to Russia."

In my view these were wild claims. Nevertheless news outlets reported them without substantiation. Even respected Western news outlets carried the nonsense. But the claims turned out to be baseless, and now have been proven wrong.

My way of uncovering the truth was to contact the Thames Valley Police, in whose jurisdiction Berezovsky died. Considering he might have been choked to death by someone, I wondered whether he died by asphyxiation. Is that what the coroner declared as the cause of death? The answer came back, "No, he has ruled the cause of death was from injuries consistent with hanging; this is not the same as asphyxiation."

But couldn't strangulation be confused with hanging? There were those news reports claiming he had bruises on his neck, and that a scarf lay on the floor near his body. But the police responded, "There is a clear difference between strangulation and hanging. The coroner has ruled the injuries are consistent with hanging, not strangulation."

That clarification should put an end to the false reports of murder, at least given what is presently known. A final conclusion must await the completion of the investigation.

Then there was the issue of death by natural causes. The *New York Times* claimed that "the stress of the last few months had brought on a fatal heart attack," attributing only "a person with knowledge of the details." The *Telegraph* chimed in too, reporting "Demyan Kudryavtsev, a business associate of the tycoon, dismissed claims that he had committed suicide, saying he had died from heart failure."

The coroner in the Royal Borough of

Windsor and Maidenhead, within which jurisdiction the autopsy was conducted, has an answer for those allegations. It comes from their standard procedures. They say if "death was due to natural causes, then no Inquest is required." But, "if the Coroner establishes that death was not due to natural causes, then he is obliged to hold an Inquest." An inquest in the death of Berezovsky is scheduled to begin on March 28. That seems to put to rest the false reports of a heart-attack death.

The media frenzy surrounding Berezovsky's death is reminiscent of that which was touched off by the mysterious 2006 death of Alexander Litvinenko. It too was full of wild, unsupported accusations.

In fact, the death of Berezovsky leaves the Litvinenko case hanging: Berezovsky was probably the most vocal source on Litvinenko's death. The Western media apparently believed his accusations against Putin. Little effort was made to check out Berezovsky's claims.

The result was another instance where media stories don't match up with numerous facts. A closer examination shows that Berezovsky had fabricated an intricate story, and that it was spread worldwide by media organizations. The media kept repeating Berezovsky's allegations that Vladimir Putin ordered the poisoning. They seemed to ignore that Berezovsky was in effect the main witness, and that he offered no facts.

Even though the coroner hadn't found Litvinenko's death to be a homicide, two Russian citizens were subsequently accused of murder. Since there were no facts revealed, the prosecutor's case appears to have been founded entirely upon Berezovsky's phony media stories.

Curiously, the prosecutor in charge, after leaving office, told the *New York Times* that he has the "gravest suspicions" of Moscow's involvement in the Litvinenko case. That speaks volumes to the substance of the case. Surely grave suspicions do not equal evidence.

But we may never know the true story. The British government is seeking to impose secrecy on relevant documents. Some allege the purpose is to suppress evidence that may prove damaging to the British government, such as ties between Berezovsky, Litvinenko, and the British secret services. The coroner has even imposed press censorship, threatening media outlets with contempt of court.

Meanwhile, there was something else missed by the bulk of the press. It is that Berezovsky died one day after the deadline passed for him to submit his witness statement to inquest officials on Litvinenko's case. It's unknown whether he complied. I asked the coroner's office if he did. But they responded, refusing to comment. The coroner actually seems to have lost control of the proceedings. A February 27th hearing appeared dominated by parties associated with Berezovsky.

Now the British authorities are left without the godfather of their Litvinenko case. This would be a good time for them to abandon the foolish prosecution that they undertook on false premises and dismiss the case. It would also be a good time for media outlets to ferret out the truth and present a fact-based account.

Let's hope that in the Berezovsky case the coroner will operate with greater speed, transparency, and integrity than his

counterpart in the Litvinenko matter, and
that the media will start utilizing greater
diligence in distinguishing wild,
unsupported claims from the verifiable facts.

Berezovsky Murdered by Journalists?
April 2, 2013

The role of journalists in the controversial Berezovsky death story.

Did you hear that on Friday, March 22, at 7:00 PM, Boris Berezovsky was visited at home by two MI6 British intelligence agents? A well-connected source gave me that information. This was the evening before Berezovsky was discovered dead in his bathroom. He was the notorious Russian robber baron who was being shielded by political asylum in London. You probably didn't see anything about the MI6 visit in the news media. But why not?

Did you know police stated that third party involvement in Berezovsky's death can not be completely eliminated? Doesn't that leave open the possibility that Berezovsky was killed by rogue journalists wishing to create a sensational story?

I'm not seriously suggesting that Berezovsky was physically murdered by these journalists. What they did was to murder the news story. Their reporting was that bad. They played up highly speculative allegations that weren't backed up by facts. Their speculation was as well sourced as my facetious allegation that Berezovsky was murdered by the journalists.

Here are some examples.

An *Irish Independent* headline read, "No suicide, says Litvinenko's wife." Did they tell us how she knew? No.

The *Guardian* quoted Nikolai Glushkov, a person identified as a friend of Berezovsky: "I'm definite Boris was killed. I have quite different information from what is being published in the media." After hearing an account from Berezovsky's ex-wife Galina, he remarked, "A scarf was there. There were traces of him being strangled around the neck." The implication seemed to be that the scarf was used in the death by someone other than Berezovsky. But no evidence was presented.

The *Mail* reported that former politician Sergei Markov said "the tycoon was assassinated because he knew too much about Western plots to undermine Putin and planned to trade this knowledge for a return to Russia." And did the *Mail* present facts to back up that one? No.

Why would the *Independent* present the wild claim of Mrs. Litvinenko's? She was untruthful before about her husband's involvement with British intelligence services. Why report what she says now about something which she has no visible means of knowing?

Similarly, it is befuddling that the *Guardian* came out with the strangulation story. I asked the police what they had to say about it. They replied, "There is a clear difference between strangulation and hanging. The coroner has ruled the injuries are consistent with hanging, not strangulation." If the *Guardian* had taken the time to ask the police, they could have avoided running with the poorly-thought-out story of strangulation.

And the *Mail*'s assassination plot story? Where is there one scintilla of evidence that Markov's comments were not just a pipe dream?

CNN ran one doozy of story by Christiane

Amanpour. She presented an interview that advanced the notion Berezovsky had been suffocated. A quick call to the police could have avoided that piece of unreliable reporting getting on air. I asked the police about that one too. A quick response came telling me the coroner "has ruled the cause of death was from injuries consistent with hanging; this is not the same as asphyxiation." Couldn't CNN have made the call too?

My hint that Berezovsky may have been visited by MI6 the evening before he was found dead was based on just one source. As such, it doesn't constitute an established fact journalistically.

But consider this:

Item: Were there functioning security cameras in Berezovsky's house and at points of entrance? I asked the police. They refused to answer. Then I asked a criminal justice expert with experience in the UK how to interpret that refusal. He said, "Such an answer is usually given when the police department (1) has the footage; (2) wants to avoid further questions about it; (3) is investigating its content; and/or (4) wants to suppress the content." Could the video reveal a visitor who confronted Berezovsky with information that precipitated a suicide? Or could it contain clues to a homicide suspect's identity? Or did it reveal the identity of some visitor that the police or British government wants to keep under wraps? Maybe some guys from MI6? Journalists haven't reported on the police secrecy about cameras, or the possible implications. Did they even ask about the cameras?

Item: March 22nd was also the day of Berezovsky's deadline to submit witness testimony to the coroner investigating the 2006 death in London of reputed former spy Alexander Litvinenko. I asked the coroner's office whether he actually submitted his testimony. They responded with a refusal to comment. Why the secrecy here? The coroner was investigating Berezovsky's possible culpability in Litvinenko's death. Does that have something to do with their refusal to comment?

Item: What did the British agents tell Berezovsky when and if they came calling? Could that have influenced his state of mind and precipitated a suicide?

These all represent things that should have been looked into. The media did do a lot of reporting on Berezovsky's state of mind. But instead of pursuing actual evidence, they came out with the story that he was depressed and despondent over financial losses. But what financial losses were there to wipe out Berezovsky's reported billions? What's the source for the allegation he was broke?

There is clearly evidence out there that contradicts the "broke" story. Earlier it was widely reported that Berezovsky received a settlement in a law suit. He had made a claim against the assets of his late associate Badri Patarkatsishvili. Potentially he could have gotten over $1 billion from that. More recently, the *Sunday Times*, to its credit, reported, "Berezovsky was in line for a cash bonanza of £200m shortly before he died, according to legal documents." So, broke? Where did other media outlets get that story from?

There is a litany of other things, as well. Was the body clothed the same as described by a *Forbes* magazine journalist who interviewed Berezovsky the previous day? There's a discrepancy in police reports of when he was last seen alive. What about that? And what about the bodyguard who discovered the body? Has anyone interviewed him? Even knowing if an interview was refused would be worth knowing. Indeed, where is that bodyguard now?

In the usual practice of journalism, a journalist gathers information and then tells his or her audience what is known. But in a large number of stories about Berezovsky's death, journalists have focused on telling audiences what the journalists don't know. For example there was the issue of the radiological examination of the premises. That was the lead of so many stories. Comparisons were drawn to the Litvinenko radiation poisoning incident. But nobody knew of any concrete connection between the cases. It was journalism by innuendo. There never was any official suggestion that radiation was involved in the death. The radiological team was there as a precaution because the dosimeter of a medical responder went off, apparently in error.

And there was a lot of buzz that the police were holding out the possibility that Berezovsky was murdered. I don't know, maybe he was. But the news media distorted what the police were saying. For instance, the *Mirror* wrote, "Murder was not ruled out today after an inquest heard that exiled Russian Boris Berezovsky was found lying in his bathroom with a ligature around his neck." That's a patently false assertion. Murder is not under consideration because of the ligature around the neck. The police simply said they couldn't completely exclude murder until all outstanding forensic and toxicological tests have been concluded. That's a very different story.

The *Mirror* comes off looking like a fun house mirror. The paper's distorted reportage is a prime example of how journalists have murdered the Berezovsky story.

In Death Berezovsky Makes Fools of Media
April 5, 2013

Whatever happened to investigative journalism?

April opened with two predominant news stories about Boris Berezovsky, the fugitive Russian robber baron who was found dead near London on March 23.

The *first* is typified by the headline "Berezovsky's girlfriend casts doubt on suicide." It ran in GlobalPost.com, based on an Agence France-Presse dispatch. The basis of the story is a purported comment of a young woman, 44 years Berezovsky's junior, who is described in media reports variously as his girlfriend or partner.

She told the Russian publication *New Times* that she hadn't seen Berezovsky since last November. Yet she has been quoted widely by news organizations such as the *Telegraph*, SkyNews, and the *Irish Independent* as an authoritative source. Some of them included a photo of her apparently in her underwear.

Why would any honest journalist believe that this 23-year-old girlfriend's observation from afar shed any light on the serious question of Berezovsky's death?

The police said he died by hanging, and that they found no evidence that any third party was involved.

Second, there was the story of a tribute purportedly written by Berezovsky's 8-year-old daughter. It was published on the website of the police department, and widely replicated by news organizations. In the tribute, the daughter said that she didn't know her father very well. The text went on to say, "His life was a turbulent roller coaster with never ending ordeals, and I admire the way in which he handled them with utter grace, control and most commendably honesty."

Does that sound like even the most precocious 8 year old to you? The use of abstraction and metaphor doesn't sound like that of an 8 year old to me. It seems out of place, and made me wonder who really wrote it.

But it turns out the tribute was not written

by an 8 year old after all. The daughter in question is well into her teen years, and certainly could have authored that tribute. But why did media outlets go with the story that such a sophisticated tribute was written by someone they believed to be 8 years old? What were they thinking? It seems to be an example of multiple media outlets compounding a mistake made somewhere along the line.

This tribute flap reminded me of the deathbed statement of Alexander Litvinenko. He was the reputed Russian spy who died in London in 2006. The deathbed statement was first reported to have been dictated to Berezovsky ally Alexander Goldfarb. In it Litvinenko said, "But as I lie here I can distinctly hear the beating of the wings of the angel of death... You may succeed in silencing one man but the howl of protest from around the world will reverberate, Mr. Putin, in your ears for the rest of your life."

It sounds eloquent, but Litvinenko did not speak English that well. His command of the language was insufficient to use the abstraction and metaphor that is expressed. But media outlets didn't question that apparent conflict, either.

Later, Goldfarb confessed that those words were not Litvinenko's. Goldfarb was now saying he wrote the statement.

Some investigative journalist should look into these issues. But are there any true investigative journalists working on the Berezovsky story? The quotes I've cited regarding the girlfriend and tribute stories seem to speak otherwise.

Last Chance for Litvinenko Coroner
July 10, 2013

Will this case finally straighten up and fly right?

A showdown is coming Friday, July 12, in the Alexander Litvinenko death case. It will occur at a hearing chaired by coroner Sir Robert Owen. This disgraced coroner will have perhaps his last chance to mitigate the damage he's already done to his own reputation.

Litvinenko is a reputed former KGB spy who died suspiciously in London in 2006. Owen became coroner last fall when the original coroner was dismissed over a scandal that had engulfed him.

Now Owen's handling of the case has resulted in the eruption of yet another scandal. At its heart is Owen's refusal to perform the duties he was retained for. His responsibility is to determine what caused the death of Litvinenko. Was it polonium poisoning as has been widely reported in the press? Or was thallium the agent of poisoning as many other media reports have claimed? Or was it something else?

Surely in the nearly seven intervening years it should have been possible to get to the bottom of this and rule on the cause of death.

Or was it found that the cause is scientifically indeterminable? If so, that information should not be kept secret. It's high time for some transparency in this case. Litvinenko's widow and son deserve to know the cause of death now, not later.

But instead of focusing on his proper job of ruling on the cause and manner of death, Owen has been conducting an illicit criminal investigation under the guise of a coroner's inquest. The British rules for coroners specifically forbid that kind of activity.

In addition to looking for the cause of death, coroners are charged with a responsibility for ruling on the manner of death. Was it a homicide, a suicide, an accident? Or is there insufficient evidence to know? In the case of a homicide, the matter of who is responsible for the death is outside of the coroner's responsibilities.

Owen has nevertheless persisted in his self-styled criminal detective work. It is unclear what his motive is. He is a high court judge who is facing mandatory retirement next year. Some speculate this is his last case, and that he wants to inflate its significance beyond that of ordinary coroner's work, albeit on a high profile coronial case. But pursuing a rogue criminal investigation seems to make it more likely that his career will end in failure and disrepute.

After media reports exposed Owen's rogue criminal work, he concocted a scheme to legitimize what he was doing. He wrote to the Lord Chancellor, head of the Justice Ministry, requesting that his hunt for criminal culpability be transferred to a different venue, one that would not have the legal restriction that is imposed on coroners regarding criminality. The Ministry quickly responded, promising an answer by July 3.

That was a crafty initiative on Owen's part. However it served to deepen the scandal. That's because his letter to the Lord Chancellor requesting the change offered facts that aren't factual. The misleading information presented by Owen centers on a statement purportedly made by Litvinenko about "those whom he suspects of being responsible for his death." But that so-called deathbed statement has been long known to have been a hoax. The hoaxer has even confessed.

Once Owen's fabrication came out in media reports, the Justice Ministry promptly notified Owen that they would not be making a decision about the requested transfer "anytime soon." The Lord Chancellor has apparently seen through Owen's ruse.

Friday's hearing will show whether or not Owen is willing to stop thumbing his nose at British law, to cease trying to drag other officials like the Lord Chancellor into his scheme, and to start performing his assigned duties. If he has scientific evidence on the cause of death, he should disclose it and enter a ruling. Likewise regarding the manner of death. Or if the evidence simply isn't there, he should honestly admit it and rule that the case is indeterminate, and close it once and for all. This may be his last chance to save even a modicum of dignity for himself.

UK Government Rebukes Litvinenko Coroner
July 20, 2013

Litvinenko coroner caught conducting illicit criminal investigation.

Coroner Sir Robert Owen was taken to the woodshed by the British government. At issue is his conduct of the inquest into the death of Alexander Litvinenko. A reputed former KGB spy, Litvinenko died suspiciously in London in 2006.

Owen's rebuke came as a result of the course he had charted for himself in investigating Litvinenko's death. The coroner's statutory responsibility, according to Home Secretary Theresa May, is to "ascertain who the deceased was, and how, when, and where he came by his death." But Owen was not focusing on those issues; he was not doing his job.

Instead, Owen had been conducting a rogue criminal investigation, looking for Russian state involvement in the death. The late Boris Berezovsky, a fugitive Russian oligarch who had been hiding out in London, had accused Russian president Vladimir Putin of culpability. He never presented any evidence, however. But Owen was apparently picking up where Berezovsky left off.

The Home Secretary reined in Owen, pointing out that he had overstepped his bounds. She stated that the law does not allow a coroner to determine criminal liability.

Earlier news reports uncovered the fact of Owen's illicit criminal investigation. In response, he concocted a scheme to transfer his work to a different venue, one without the restrictions placed on coroners regarding openness and criminality. It was a clever strategy.

But when Owen wrote to the government requesting the transfer, he misrepresented the circumstances of the case. He said, "It is a highly exceptional situation when the victim of what appears to have been a murder is interviewed by police before he dies, and makes a public statement in which he names those whom he suspects of being responsible for his death..."

However, the public record shows that

Litvinenko made no such statement to the police. It is true that there was a written public statement accusing Putin that was attributed to Litvinenko. It was released after his death. But that document has been shown to be a fraud. The statement was a hoax, and the hoaxer has publically confessed.

At last count, the Litvinenko inquest has spent over $2 million of British taxpayer money. Despite all the flurry of activity created by Owen, there does not seem to have been any progress toward establishing the cause and manner of death. The work thus far seems to have been a complete waste of money.

What more will it take for the coroner to rule on the specific circumstances? Secretary May called Litvinenko's death an "apparent murder." Was it indeed a homicide? Or was it a suicide or accident? It is hard to understand why the coroner could not have ruled on that long ago.

Likewise on the cause of death. Many media reports claim that radioactive polonium was the agent of death. Other reports say the cause was thallium poisoning. It should be possible to answer this question with scientific evidence. Either there is evidence, or there isn't.

Litvinenko's death happened nearly seven years ago. If sufficient evidence is not on hand, perhaps it is time to admit that the cause and manner of death are indeterminable, and then simply close the case. Why spend more British taxpayer money to accomplish nothing?

Litvinenko: Massive Media Fraud Uncovered
July 23, 2013

News reports about the Litvinenko case are demonstrably false and unreliable.

Did you hear that Great Britain has abandoned justice in favor of international politics in the Alexander Litvinenko case? He is the reputed former KGB spy who died mysteriously in London in 2006. If you've been reading recent news reports you likely heard of the UK's capitulation. A *New York Times* July 19 headline proclaimed, "Litvinenko Inquiry Blocked to Avoid Upsetting Russia, British Official Suggests."

What you may not have realized is that there is nothing in that headline that is true. It is an outright hoax.

The *Times* is not alone in this media fraud. Here are some other equally false variants: "Britain Says Ties with Russia Played Part in Litvinenko Ruling" (Reuters), "May [Home Secretary Theresa May] Cites Moscow Relations as Factor in Litvinenko Decision" (*Financial Times*), and "Litvinenko Inquiry

Request Refused for Fear of Alienating Russia" (*Guardian*).

These headlines simply don't comport with the facts. The media are reporting on a July 17 letter issued by Home Secretary May. In it she reprimands Litvinenko coroner Sir Robert Owen for not fulfilling his statutory responsibilities. But nowhere does she even mention Russia or Moscow, much less suggest she or her government are in fear of alienating the country. She doesn't even hint at that. The claims in the headlines I've cited are patently false. And the headline intimations that there won't be a further investigation into the death? Completely bogus, too.

Stories of collusion between the UK and Russia to thwart justice in the Litvinenko case are not new, however. Even before May's letter was sent, a July 12 *Daily Mail* headline proclaimed, "UK 'colluded' with Kremlin to block inquiry into death of poisoned Russian spy Litvinenko."

BBC chimed in, too. In a story on the same day, it quoted an observer: "There's some sort of collusion behind the scenes with Her Majesty's government and the Kremlin to obstruct justice."

Didn't the media outlets check for facts?
Indeed, are there facts to back up the
allegations?

The media outlets offered no substantiation
for the claimed collusion. A couple of sources
were cited. But the sources gave no
substantiation either. Suspiciously, they
seem to be associates of the late Boris
Berezovsky. He was a fugitive Russian
oligarch hiding out in London. By his own
admission, he had big plans to destabilize
Russia, incite bloody revolution, and throw
out the constitution. What's more, the
Berezovsky-related sources cited in the press
have demonstrated questionable credibility
themselves. Why didn't the media scrutinize
what those people were saying?

Berezovsky was a master media manipulator.
His outlandish aspirations, and the
counterfactual tales he uttered trying to
achieve them, have received serious coverage
by major media outlets around the world.
This went on for over a decade. That adds up
to a lot of journalistic malfeasance.

Alleging British-Russian collusion is a theme

that the Berezovsky clan has used repeatedly. Following a coroner's hearing in late February, a media blitz emerged contending that Russia and Britain are conspiring to suppress potentially relevant secret British documents. Attorney Ben Emmerson said the British are "dancing to the Russian tarantella." He is a lawyer widely reported to have been paid by Berezovsky to represent the widow Litvinenko.

That seems to be the modus operandi of the Berezovsky group: A hearing or a judgment doesn't go their way. Then all of a sudden there appears a barrage of news and social media stories advancing scurrilous allegations that have no apparent basis in fact. The media outlets gobble up the sensational-sounding stories without checking the facts. And the public is ill-served by a host of reports that are simply journalistic garbage.

The July 12 specious stories flooded international news in the wake of a coroner's hearing on the case. Perhaps the most prevalent of those stories is the tale of the "public inquiry." Typical headlines included "UK Refuses to Hold Public Inquiry into Litvinenko Poisoning" (Reuters), and

"Litvinenko: No Inquiry into Spy's Death" (Sky News). The *Wall Street Journal* tweeted, "UK Won't Hold Public Litvinenko Inquiry," as did the *Huffington Post*, "UK Declines to Hold Public Inquiry into Litvinenko Death."

These Berezovskyesque reports make it sound like the British government wants to put a lid on whatever it was that happened to Litvinenko. I don't know whether it does or not. But these media reports are fundamentally misleading.

You see, "Public Inquiry" doesn't mean what it sounds like. Common sense says the term means an inquiry that's out in the open. But in this case, the words are a tricky technical term. It's actually a misnomer. According to British law, a "Public" Inquiry actually can be conducted behind closed doors in secrecy. There never was any intention that the Public Inquiry be completely transparent. The media reports about this give entirely the wrong impression. I didn't see any that clarified the use of the term to set the record straight.

Either they were just witlessly going along with the Berezovsky crowd, or they didn't care enough to understand what they were reporting. Or worse.

Many of the media stories spoke as if there naturally should be a Public Inquiry. It would have been worth asking why. There have been curious deaths of people far more important in the world than Litvinenko that were not subject of a truly open or public inquiry. The Warren Commission inquiry into the death of President John F. Kennedy, for instance, was conducted primarily in closed sessions. Even Elvis Presley didn't get a public inquiry into his death. Why Litvinenko?

Right from the beginning, the Litvinenko coverage has presented a panoply of misinformation. The basic media story that Litvinenko was murdered on orders of Russian president Vladimir Putin was a fabrication of Berezovsky's. I detailed that in my book, *The Phony Litvinenko Murder*.

There is ample evidence that any stories or allegations coming from the Berezovsky clan should receive extreme scrutiny. Berezovsky himself was declared "inherently unreliable" by a British high court judge.

Berezovsky is not the only unreliable one. His right-hand man claimed Litvinenko had dictated to him a deathbed allegation fingering Putin. But it was a hoax, too. The hoaxer later confessed that the so-called deathbed statement contained his words, not Litvinenko's.

Despite all that, most media outlets continue to refer to the deathbed accusation as though it were factual. And now they are referring to a potentially secret inquiry as "public." Perhaps the final kicker is the "spy" moniker widely given Litvinenko by the media. There's no reliable evidence that Litvinenko ever did espionage work. He wasn't a spy, and he never worked for the KGB.

What is most puzzling is why any legitimate journalist would believe any story told by anyone who was a member of Berezovsky's inner circle. Are the journalists severely gullible, or corrupt, or incompetent, or do they simply not care about getting things right? Whatever the case, it is a sad commentary on the media that almost all news stories about the Litvinenko case amount to nothing more than a journalistic flimflam.

More Litvinenko Media Fraud
August 15, 2013

Who's Kidding Who?

An article titled "Litvinenko falls victim to Western security services' operations -- journalist" was distributed on August 10, by Itar-TASS.

It reports on a *Daily Mail* piece by American freelance journalist Edward Jay Epstein titled "It's the murder mystery still causing political shockwaves in London and Moscow. But was the radioactive Russian spy killed by bungling MI6 agents?"

The Voice of Russia also chimed in with its story, "Alexander Litvinenko first victim of trade in radioactive materials."

All three articles contain misinformation and serious distortions.

Some were originated by Epstein. Others were introduced by the other media organizations themselves. While these stories may contain some information that is accurate, it is hard to know what to believe, given the presence of identifiably false information. As a result, they represent reports that can't be relied upon.

An obvious tip-off to Epstein's unreliability came when he reported that Litvinenko "died leaving behind a deathbed statement he had dictated to a friend, accusing Putin of orchestrating his murder."

That so-called deathbed statement was a hoax. It's been widely reported as such. The hoaxer has even confessed that he wrote the statement himself. If Epstein missed or misunderstood that one, what else did he miss or misunderstand?

Polonium is widely alleged to have been the poison that killed Litvinenko. Epstein called Litvinenko's polonium a "nuclear weapon." Years earlier, Epstein claimed that all known deaths from polonium were results of accidents. Where's Epstein's evidence of weaponized polonium? Reports have described it as component of some bombs. Aluminum also has been reported as a bomb component. That doesn't make aluminum a nuclear weapon.

That's not the only instance of Epstein being

apparently self-contradictory. In his *Daily Mail* piece he said that a full inquest "isn't to be heard until next year." But at the same time he told the Voice of Russia UK Edition that "the British government has not allowed the inquest to go forward."

Epstein also writes about stockpiles of polonium. Since he calls polonium a weapon, that conjures up images of stockpiles of ammunition or missiles. But in earlier writing, Epstein claims "it cannot be stockpiled for more than a few months." "It rapidly decays..." he explained. That would make a stockpile of polonium more like a stockpile of potatoes than one of weapons, at least in terms of shelf life. This suggests quite a different image. Yet in the *Daily Mail* Epstein asserts that the Litvinenko polonium could have been "stolen from stockpiles in the former Soviet Union or in the US..."

Epstein goes on, "As for the small quantity of polonium 210 involved, it could have been made in any country with an uninspected nuclear reactor -- a list that in 2006 included Russia, Britain, China, France, India, Israel, Pakistan, and North Korea." That's suggestive that the polonium was produced in a nuclear weapons program, since that's a common thread connecting those countries. "But the more likely source of the polonium, and this is a submission I make, is from an industrial or commercial application, not from a power station or nuclear weapons programme," is what the British Home Office entered into the record at a pre-inquest hearing. If Epstein has evidence to the contrary, why didn't he present it in his article?

What Itar-TASS and Voice of Russia did was to take this bad story and make it worse.

The Itar-TASS lead sentence says that British security services might have played a role in the death, with attribution to Epstein. They quote him, "What I found led me to conclude that the accepted version of events is far from being the true story and raised a tantalizing question: could the British secret service be to blame?"

That's their scoop? It's just a tantalizing question, not even a developed theory. And actually it is old news. Back in November of last year the Litvinenko coroner said he was considering "the possible culpability of the British state in the death of Alexander Litvinenko." The Itar-TASS article even reports on the pre-inquest hearing at which the coroner made that statement. The article said the coroner might look into involvement of Berezovsky, Chechens, and the Spanish mafia. But they left the British government off the list. I guess if they had included it, readers could have seen that their scoop was indeed no scoop.

The Voice of Russia did its part to further confuse the issue. Its headline claimed that Litvinenko was the "first victim of trade in radioactive materials." But the article doesn't mention any trade at all. Perhaps the VoR writer was thinking of Epstein's former analysis of the case. In 2008 he wrote, "After considering all the evidence, my hypothesis is that Litvinenko came in contact with a polonium-210 smuggling operation and was, either wittingly or unwittingly, exposed to it." Epstein has apparently now backed away from that conclusion without offering an explanation.

The VoR story also stated: "It is understood that Litvinenko worked for British, US, and Italian secret services." He was working for the US now? Epstein didn't say that. It was gratuitously added by VoR. What Epstein actually said is that "Litvinenko was involved with a number of intelligence services..." And his involvement with the CIA? According to Epstein, they "rejected his offer to defect in 2000." And that constitutes working for US secret services?

So what is Epstein's current analysis of the Litvinenko case? Now he says, "My belief is that the strange, radioactive death of Alexander Litvinenko is likely to earn its place in the annals of unsolved crime for ever."

Actually, I agree with that analysis, and have been reporting my conclusion in articles since April 2012. This is a radioactive contamination case that itself has become contaminated by false information. There is so much deception that has been introduced into this case by so many different parties and to serve varied agendas, that it is hard for me to imagine that the truth is actually knowable.

What Klutz Handles Putin's PR?
September 25, 2013

Will anyone ever take credit for the disaster?

When Russian president Vladimir Putin proposed a plan to avert American bombing of Syria, president Obama gave it a green light. But critics claim that was a big mistake. Putin has an ulterior motive they say.

But what if the exact same plan had been proposed by former president Jimmy Carter? Would he be suspected of evil intent, too? Of course not. The difference lies in the reputations of the two. Carter is viewed largely as a do-gooding former leader. Putin is thought of as a ruthless dictator who will stop at nothing.

It's worth asking what Putin has done to earn such a dark reputation. The answer lies in what's been revealed about him through the news media. For instance: he launched a brutal invasion of Georgia, cracked down on the free press that Yeltsin nurtured, and ordered the murder of reputed former spy

Alexander Litvinenko in London.

The problem with these and many other accusations is that they lack a factual basis. Indeed, as incredible as it may seem, the stories were fabrications of Putin's political enemies, such as the late Boris Berezovsky.

The facts show Georgia was the aggressor in the Georgia-Russia war, according to an EU investigation. There was no free press from the Yeltsin era for Putin to crack down on. Yeltsin era laws precluded media business profitability and independence. The media never were free to just serve the needs of their audiences. And Litvinenko? In the almost seven years since his suspicious death, the London Coroner has yet to rule whether or not the death was even a homicide. The story that Putin did it was concocted by Berezovsky as yet another way to damage Putin's reputation.

If the truth has been on Putin's side, how could his enemies have succeeded in destroying his reputation so thoroughly?

Putin's political enemies effectively weaponized the media to attack his reputation. That's how. They engaged in highly sophisticated media manipulation. And Putin put up no defense. He let them get away with it.

If this had been an actual military attack, there would be a top general charged with defending Russia's homeland. What about a media attack? Who's in charge? That would be Dmitry Peskov, Putin's press secretary and communications director. He's in charge of Putin's PR. But, this problem requires more than just PR to effectuate change.

Right now the Kremlin is ill-prepared for the challenge. Maybe it simply does not know what to do or how to respond. But if things are to change for the better, the Kremlin had better seek outside technical expertise with a track record for turning around the kind of reputational disasters that it faces. This needs to be done now not later.

It is widely reported that the Kremlin turned to the American PR firm Ketchum for help. Some say Ketchum has been paid $40 million all told. Peskov has denied that. Privately I've been told the Kremlin believes that paying to protect Putin's image is a shameful thing. That's a counterproductive belief that it should abandon quickly.

But what has Ketchum accomplished?. It has openly admitted to having placed Putin's famous op-ed in the *New York Times*. That's the one that gave Obama "friendly" advice about Syria, and questioned the idea of American "exceptionalism." That all turned into a fiasco. The whole thing blew up in their faces. And Putin caught the flack.

The problem with that op-ed initiative is twofold. First of all, Putin does not have the credibility with the American people or with their political leaders to be offering any kind of constructive advice. Given the widespread misconceptions about the Russian leader, it is ludicrous to think that his audience would regard his comments as anything but ridiculous.

The second issue is Putin's attack on American exceptionalism. That was an ill-chosen and inappropriate target. All that the usual rhetoric on "American exceptionalism" amounts to is an attempt by American leaders to help Americans feel good about themselves and their country. There's nothing wrong with that. Putin made the same kind of overture himself to Russians when he first ran for president. He offered to help Russians to feel better about themselves and about their country, especially after the troubling decade they had just lived through.

This technique is not used only by national leaders. Membership organizations use it. So do magazine editors. It's basically a means for promoting good feelings through a sense of solidarity among a constituency. Of course they don't all call it American exceptionalism. Each has its own term for it. But it's basically all the same process.

What I think Putin was really trying to get at, and what would have been a far more successful target for him, is the assertions of so many American political leaders that the United States has a manifest destiny to be the world's self-defined moral militia. That would have been a better target.

But now the net effect of Ketchum's deft work in placing that questionable op-ed is that Putin was subjected to widespread ridicule and criticism. Ketchum didn't make Putin look better. It made him look like he was virtually committing PR suicide.

Putin's reputation couldn't be worse now. For years he has been maligned over and over again. At this point, if someone were to simply tell the truth about Putin, it would not be believed. It would be counterintuitive, given all the past misinformation. The situation is so bad that if Putin were to find a cure for cancer, he'd risk being vilified for it.

Ketchum may have the capability for getting an op-ed placed in a major newspaper. But it certainly hasn't demonstrated that it is up to the challenge of dealing with Putin's reputational problems.

What a predicament that places Putin in. Putin relied on Ketchum to be in effect his "general" for the defense of his reputation. It was unprepared for such a technical job. Placing op-eds in Western newspapers is kid stuff compared to what that needs to be done.

Ever since Putin became Yeltsin's prime minister, I've studied carefully the media attacks that have beset him. I've identified the various methodologies that have been used. Frankly, the attacks have been very well done. They are timely, sophisticated, and highly effective. Neither Ketchum nor Kremlin staff can match that expertise and sophistication.

There is a Russian and American initiative that I strongly endorse that has the capability to rehabilitate Putin's image and protect it from future attacks. It uses cutting-edge techniques, not old-time PR. I think this could remediate Putin's problem decisively.

But it's been hard to get this proposal past the palace guard, so to speak. And when finally brought to the attention of Putin, he had no response. Perhaps he has no positive expectations for it based on his past PR failures. But if he wants a changed reputational outcome, he'll have to consider the new approach.

The Sochi Olympics in February 2014 stand out as a prominent opportunity for doing further damage to Putin's reputation, not to mention how it could harm Russia's national interests in general.

Many of the past media attacks have been staged opportunistically. Some have occurred while Putin has been at highly-visible international events. One was even orchestrated on his birthday.

When it comes to opportunities for further

tarnishing Putin's image, the Olympics are a real plum. Anti-Putin media manipulation is already underway in the windup toward February. And that's just the start.

Putin claims to have high hopes that the Olympics will contribute positively to Russia's international image. However, his political enemies very well may turn the tables on him once again and succeed at inflicting more harm.

If Putin seriously wants a good PR outcome from the Olympics, and hopes for the games to give Russia a boost internationally, time is running short. He's got to act decisively and address the currently dilapidated state of his international reputation in an efficacious way.

While the Olympics offer Putin's political enemies an opportunity to inflict further harm, they also offer Putin an opportunity to take a totally different approach to reputational management and remediation. I'm talking about something more cutting-edge than past efforts.

If Putin fails to seize this opportunity, the unfortunate consequences may stand out for all to see.

History is littered with conspicuous examples of how grave, unaddressed misunderstandings have led to tremendous calamities in the world.

Britain Cans Case Against Russia
January 2, 2014

The UK government finally capitulates.

It's the end of a rogue witch-hunt. The
mysterious 2006 death in London of reputed
former spy Alexander Litvinenko is at issue.
Coroner Sir Robert Owen had been
exhaustively looking for possible Russian
state culpability. Then suddenly he stopped
looking. On December 18, he issued a formal
ruling that removed the Russian issue from
the scope of his inquest.

That is an extremely startling development.
Previously, Owen had said that the possible
culpability of the Russian state was of central
importance in the case. Much of Owen's
work had been focused on finding a Russian
culprit.

Now suddenly he's given up. This seems to
represent a veritable implosion of his case.

News reports immediately attributed this
collapse to the British government's refusal
to allow consideration of secret government
documents in the case. But that's a bogus

explanation. It may be face-saving for Owen. It's also face-saving for the media.

The phony explanation likely arose because all parties had been entangled in a case-related misadventure that dates back to 2011. It involves the glaring illegitimacy of the coroner's pursuit of a culprit. Owen pretended he was conducting a proper investigation. The media pretended the same. But the truth lay elsewhere. Owen, in effect, had been on a fishing expedition, but with no license to fish.

You see, British law specifically forbids coroners from determining criminal liability. That's a job for police and prosecutors. The idea that the coroner should take the lead is a fabrication that was enthusiastically advanced by associates of the late Boris Berezovsky, a fugitive Russian business tycoon who had been hiding out in London. Litvinenko had been in Berezovsky's employ originally in Moscow and later in London.

It was Berezovsky and his followers who kicked off the story that Russian president Vladimir Putin was behind the purported spy's murder. The only trouble is this was a murder case without a murder and a spy drama without a spy.

The Berezovsky clan offered no facts, just specious allegations. There's no evidence that Litvinenko ever did espionage work, and the London Coroner has never declared his death to be a murder. And Putin's involvement? No evidence either. But there is a lot to substantiate that Berezovsky was out to get Putin for a long time.

It can be shown that Berezovsky and his followers made up the popularized Litvinenko story. And the gullible media gobbled up all the baloney. And apparently so did Owen.

To promote an end to Owen's witch-hunt misadventure, "Russia without Spin," a private sector initiative that I strongly support, embarked upon an intervention aimed at cutting through the nonsense. It was undertaken as a demonstration of the efficacy of the RwS's proprietary skills in counteracting news reports founded upon fabricated information. The Litvinenko case was ideal for that purpose.

Working through a few cooperating media outlets and by providing carefully-crafted analyses that reached the Justice Ministry, the Home Office, and the High Court, the intervention project picked apart Owen's activities, one by one.

Meanwhile, Owen tried to connive and misrepresent in order to protect his witch-hunt. He attempted to overrule the government's national security objections to the release of secret documents. But the High Court quashed his action, accusing him of making "an error of law." It also acknowledged receiving a submission that Owen had "mischaracterized the nature and extent of his duty in conducting the inquest."

Owen also tried to set up a sham "Public Inquiry" to get his hands on the secret documents. Now, mind you, these documents were not needed for Owen to fulfill his coronial responsibilities. He only wanted them to further his rogue criminal investigation. Coroners are principally supposed to rule on the cause and manner of death. But Owen was refusing to do that job.

Home Secretary Theresa May reined in Owen in his request for a so-called Public Inquiry. She said it wasn't needed. At the same time, she reprimanded him for not doing his proper job. May told Owen that his duty is to "ascertain who the deceased was, and how, when and where he came by his death." May added that "'how' in this context means 'by what means' and not 'in what broad circumstances.'" In other words: no witch-hunt for a culprit.

In the end, the Russia without Spin's intervention proved successful. Owen's case against Russia didn't really implode. What happened was actually more of a controlled demolition. It ended the rogue investigation Owen was conducting, what with all its extensive media exposure. Hopefully, Owen will now heed Secretary May's admonition, and will start performing his statutory duties.

A remaining victim in all this is the widow Litvinenko. Since her husband's death, she has been crying out for justice in the case. She wants to know, and deserves to know, what happened to her husband. Mrs. Litvinenko made it clear that she was looking toward the coroner to deliver that justice.

Clearly the actions of the Berezovsky clan, Owen, and Andrew Reid, Owen's coronial predecessor, gave Mrs. Litvinenko reason to expect that the coroner could provide her with an answer. They should have explained that the coroner is not allowed to assign culpability. The coronial process does not include a prosecution and defense. Neither would a so-called Public Inquiry. So even if Owen had been allowed to finger a Russian suspect, that person would have had no opportunity for a defense. What kind of justice would that have been?

Personally, I think that Owen owes Mrs. Litvinenko an enormous apology. It's the least he could do.

Sadly, Mrs. Litvinenko may never get a clear answer about what happened to her husband. Since his tragic death, figures such as Berezovsky and Owen have muddied the waters so thoroughly with fabricated allegations on Berezovsky's part and false promises of justice by Owen, that it is hard to envision an honest and conclusive outcome. Lamentably, the record has been utterly contaminated. It's doubtful that even the long-sought-after secret documents are free of Berezovsky's fabricated nonsense.

Sochi Under Attack by US
January 13, 2014

We told you so!

The United States has unleashed its heavy
artillery on the Sochi Olympics. It's in the
form of an official Travel Alert to Americans
issued by the Department of State. It says US
citizens "should remain attentive regarding
their personal security at all times." The
Alert justifies itself with a litany of potential
problems that under scrutiny turn out to be
largely non-issues. This has all the
appearances of a scare tactic.

It may cause a lot of Americans to reconsider
attending. A *New York Times* headline
warned, "Americans Traveling to Winter
Games Cautioned." President Barack Obama
already announced that he isn't going.

Previously, many potshots have been taken
at the upcoming Olympics in media reports
from various outlets. They too raised fears
about attending the Games. But the new US
actions aren't merely potshotting. This is a
frontal attack with big cannons.

All this comes in the wake of two highly-publicized terrorist events. The first was a series of two suicide bombings in Volgograd, Russia in late December. The second was the discovery of six dead bodies in cars on the outskirts of Pyatigorsk, Russia in early January.

Regarding the former, a CBS News report read, "Suicide bomber attacks near Sochi." CNN's version said, "Russia bombings raise questions about Sochi Olympics security."

On the Pyatigorsk incident, ABC News proclaimed, "Mystery bodies, explosives discovered near Winter Olympics site." The *Atlanta Journal Constitution* reported, "Russia launches probe after six found dead near Sochi."

These were certainly tragic events. But the media should have paid a bit more attention to their geography. For instance, would a suicide bombing in the Italian Alps be a realistic worry for people at a large public gathering in Berlin, Germany? Or likewise an incident 100 miles north of Montreal to people in New York City? Those are examples of distances similar to the expanse between Volgograd and Sochi. That's what

CBS news called "close."

In the other example, Pyatigorsk to Sochi? That's like Brooklyn, New York to Brattleboro, Vermont, or Munich, Germany to Alsace, France. ABC News and the *Atlanta Journal Constitution* both considered that proximity to be "near."

It's hard to imagine that journalists and editors at these media outlets are simply out to lunch. I find it difficult to chalk-up these exaggerations to ignorance. I'd call them potshots.

Then there's the State Department's cannon blast. The Travel Alert. Certainly, travelers should always be "attentive regarding their personal security" wherever they travel. It just makes sense. But why did the State Department make that the subject of an ominous sounding Travel Alert?

For comparison, I checked to see if similar alerts are active for other places in the world. What I found is that there are currently two. One is for Egypt over the "continuing political and social unrest," and the other for Madagascar, related to its election season. It's because, "gatherings intended to be peaceful can turn violent with little or no warning."

But the general instability in those two troubled countries is a far cry from the security-controlled environment that will be present at the Sochi Olympics complex. Indeed, wouldn't security and control be bywords of any Olympic venue past and future?

The United States had the experience of hosting the Salt Lake City Olympics in 2002. That was just five months after the 9/11 attacks on New York and Washington. I searched for press coverage from the months preceding the opening of those Games. Who in the United States believed at that time that the al-Qaeda threat had been eliminated? I went looking for reportage regarding any suggested Olympic danger. There wasn't too much. NPR reported on February 7, 2002, "When the Winter Olympics gets under way in Salt Lake City Friday, officials promise the heaviest security ever for a sporting event." (Keep in mind that the earlier terrorist activities killed about 3000 people.) But, in contrast, on December 30, 2013, NPR carried this report: "Two suicide bombings in as many days have killed 31 people and raised concerns that Islamic militants have begun a terrorist campaign in Russia that could stretch into the Sochi Olympics in February."

Notice how the 2002 report has a reassuring tone, whereas the 2013 report seems alarmist. The tonal difference in coverage seems to belie the relative death totals. What is NPR up to?

There's no doubt that the Sochi Olympics presents a unique security challenge. And disasters at previous Olympics show there is a concrete risk of tragedy. But the media have failed to take into account that Putin's political enemies have been taunting him with suggestions of violence during his showpiece Olympics and urging boycotts. There's been little investigative journalism to differentiate between credible physical threats and the use of verbal threats in the media as a weapon. Overall, the news coverage that I've seen seems to suggest a goal of fomenting alarm, instead of simply reporting the facts.

No one should be surprised that media-based attacks against Russia and its leader would grow stronger during the Olympic season. Past media attacks, organized by Putin's political enemies, have been opportunistic and also founded upon fabricated allegations. Crusading journalist Anna Politkovskaya was killed on Putin's birthday. The initial media blitz over reputed former spy Alexander Litvinenko's poisoning in London occurred while Putin was attending the Asia Pacific Economic Cooperation Summit in Hanoi. The focus of the attendant news stories involved accusations of Putin's culpability. The Sochi Olympics now present Putin's enemies with an obvious opportunity for doing similar damage to his reputation. Strangely, Putin has never done anything to effectively counteract the incessant malicious media attacks against him.

As early as October 2012, efforts were made to draw the Kremlin's attention to the impending Olympics media problem. Russia without Spin, a Russian-American private sector initiative that I strongly support, was offering to help with its specialized expertise. But it was hard to find friends in the Kremlin for this project. Those within the administration, and leaders of its communications arms, ultimately seemed not to care about solving the problem. They appeared more focused on simply assuring their share of the state budget, even though the problem of Putin's terrible international reputation would go unaddressed in any serious and effective way.

In response, Russia without Spin undertook a demonstration to show the efficacy its proprietary skills in counteracting news reports that are founded upon fabricated information. The Litvinenko case was ideal for that purpose. It involved a high-profile British search for alleged Russian culpability, albeit with an absence of any substantiating facts. In the end, the Russia without Spin project was successful in its initiative for ending the specious search. The quest for Russian culpability was cancelled and the Litvinenko topic was taken out of the news, at least for the time being.

Russia without Spin's Litvinenko demonstration, having achieved its objective, has now concluded its work. The Litvinenko story may flare up again in the future. But it's unclear what if anything the Putin administration would do in response. The Russia without Spin initiative still stands ready to help, however, if called upon.

Perhaps now it's time for the Kremlin to reassess its interest in remediating its reputational problems. If it does nothing, Putin and Russia will continue to be victims of the typical malicious media attacks they have sustained since the beginning of Putin's leadership in Moscow. It's hard to see how that will help anyone other than Putin's political enemies.

Chapter 7
The Fishy "Public" Inquiry

A faux trial capable of producing nothing but a bogus result.

BRITISH Prime Minister David Cameron's personal mission in 2014 to hit Russia hard over the MH17 disaster triggered a reopening of the dormant 2006 Alexander Litvinenko death case.

Apparently the goal is to unearth evidence that will appear to incriminate Putin. The newly opened Public Inquiry in reality is nothing more than a part of a geopolitical stunt.

This development is worse than a veritable kangaroo court. That kind of legal travesty is at least conducted in public. In this case the term "Public Inquiry" is a complete misnomer. It gives the impression that there will be transparency.

But under British law a so-called Public Inquiry can be conducted behind closed doors with no public accountability. Indeed, one of the rationales given when authorization for a Public Inquiry was requested was for the opportunity to operate in secret.

Multitudinous statements that this Public Inquiry will finally bring about justice in the Litvinenko case represent a perversion of the truth. The Inquiry can entertain testimony from hand-picked witnesses. They can level unsupported accusations. And accused parties have no right for cross examination. This so-called quest for justice is in itself fundamentally unjust.

A Senseless Inquiry

As you have learned by now, the mainstream news story about Litvinenko was phony. It had been a cunning fabrication perpetrated by Boris Berezovsky, the political arch enemy of Putin's.

In light of this, Cameron looks pretty foolish in reopening the witch hunt for Russian culpability. That activity had been closed down earlier when it came to light that there was no merit to the pursuit.

Now in his zeal to get at Putin over the crisis in Ukraine, Cameron allowed himself to be sucked in by an old fabricated story that has no factual basis.

A Record of Defiance and Deceit

Back in 2012, British high court judge Sir Robert Owen tried his hand at incriminating Russia over the Litvinenko matter. He had been appointed coroner in the then six-year-old unsolved death case. But ultimately he refused to perform his statutory duty to rule on how, when, and where Litvinenko came to his demise. Instead he led an intense witch hunt to pin criminal culpability, something coroners are specifically forbidden by law from doing.

When news got out of Owen's rogue activities, he attempted to outmaneuver the rules. That's when he asked the British government to convert his coroner's inquest into an official Inquiry that could be held in secret.

Home Secretary Theresa May denied Owen's request, ruling that an Inquiry is unnecessary. She told him to stop the witch hunt and concentrate on his statutory responsibilities, just as the Russia without Spin initiative had been pressing for all along.

Geopolitics Trumps Justice

Cameron's current anti-Putin crusade surprisingly has prompted May to completely reverse herself. Now she inexplicably gave Owen the Inquiry he wanted.

While last year she said that Litvinenko's widow and son "would learn no more from an Inquiry than from the Inquest," she is now saying she hopes "this Inquiry will be of some comfort to his widow Mrs. Litvinenko." That's all quite a dramatic turnabout.

A 2010 *Guardian* headline proclaimed that "Theresa May will be nobody's stooge." How embarrassing it must be for Mrs. May to have to kowtow to Cameron in his vendetta against Russia.

Her troubles are not over, though. I've seen where Owen based his request for the Inquiry on falsified facts. For instance, he claimed Litvinenko had made a public statement that fingered Putin for his death. But that purported public statement was a hoax. The hoaxer has confessed and admitted there was no factual basis for his claims.

The final insult to integrity is May's appointment of Owen to be the leader of the new Inquiry.

That flies in the face of the legal requirement for impartiality. Owen has demonstrated he's interested in one main thing -- finding Russian culpability -- and is willing to flout the law in hot pursuit.

There is no reasonable basis for considering Owen to be impartial. His own actions as coroner erased any presumption of impartiality.

Add to that his falsification of facts when he requested approval for the Inquiry. This man does not appear to be even honest, much less impartial. Owen is clearly unfit for any role in this case.

But get this: Until Owen was put on the Litvinenko case, he was facing mandatory retirement from the bench in September 2014.

Extending his activities in the Litvinenko Inquiry keeps him on the government dole indefinitely. It looks like he's milking the Litvinenko case for all it's worth to his own personal benefit.

I wonder what British taxpayers will think of that. The Litvinenko inquest has already cost them over $4 million.

How is Mrs. May going to explain all this?

And, finally, given all the foregoing, how can any outcome from the Inquiry be considered morally legitimate?

In fact any conclusion of this Inquiry should be considered a product of fakery and deception. As such conclusions of the Inquiry are totally irrelevant in any real sense.

Chapter 8
So What Have We Learned?

A review of key points to remember.

HERE'S the situation:

--The mainstream Litvinenko story started off as a fabrication concocted by mortal political enemies of Putin's.

--Their self-proclaimed goal was to promote a violent revolution in Russia and to install their own monarchical regime. No kidding. This is what Berezovsky himself has admitted to.

--Extremely sophisticated techniques were being used to build the false narrative.

--The phony Litvinenko poisoning story was foisted upon the media by Britain's top PR talent working at Berezovsky's behest.

--The media failed at due diligence and fact checking, and just ran the fabricated stories.

--When Litvinenko died, Berezovsky's people hoaxed the world with a purported deathbed accusation against Putin. Almost everyone was taken in by the hoax.

Ultimately the hoax was exposed. The hoaxer confessed that it was he who wrote the statement not Litvinenko. But the media persist in referring to Litvinenko's deathbed statement as if it were legitimate.

--While media reports called Litvinenko's death a murder, the London Coroner has never ruled it to be a homicide.

--Indeed, the coroner refused to perform his statutory responsibility to rule on the manner and cause of death.

--Instead he went rogue and in defiance of British law presided over an illicit witch hunt for Russian state culpability.

--The Russia without Spin initiative directed official attention to the outlandish activities of the rogue coroner, while also exposing the out-of-control coroner's behavior to the public.

--The Home Secretary directed Coroner Owen to cut out the inappropriate witch hunt and instead to address his statutory responsibility to rule on the manner and cause of death. This was a clear validation of the effectiveness in using the SSOPP methodology.

--But just months later British Prime Minister Cameron brought the Litvinenko case to its highest-ever level of political maneuvering. His intervention resulted in Home Secretary Theresa May's capitulation and reversal of her earlier ruling about the scope of Owen's work.

--This led to the opening of a Public Inquiry that amounts in effect to a kangaroo court that has the ability to operate in secret.

--No conclusions from a faux trial like that can ever merit any public confidence. Who can trust the fruits of an overwhelmingly corrupted process of inquiry?

Chapter 9
Case Solved!

What's the solution?

THE real solution to this case is simple:

It is to acknowledge that no reliable conclusion can be drawn about the culpability for Litvinenko's death. This essential realization neither incriminates nor exonerates anyone.

But it admits that the record has become too thoroughly confounded by lies and fabricated stories. False information has permeated the official understanding of the case. Officials have developed strongly-held beliefs that are grounded in falsehoods. And indeed the case has become politicized by the highest levels of government.

The original coroner, Andrew Reid, ruled that "the whole purpose of the inquest is to investigate the credibility of the competing theories." He was talking about the who-done-it theories.

The predominant theory has been Berezovsky's "Putin did it" fabrication.

So if the coroner is asking for credibility, it's worth questioning whether Berezovsky's theory has any credibility. He offered no proof, no evidence, only his own words. Are his words reliable?

In the Berezovsky v. Abramovich case, the High Court judge ruled that Berezovsky is "inherently unreliable." That would mean that his theory in the Litvinenko case cannot be relied upon, too. Inherent unreliability speaks about the core of the person. If one discounts Berezovsky's theory that Putin is behind Litvinenko's death, doesn't that pull the rug from under the government's case?

Given that, there's been no real need all along for the witch hunt for Russian state culpability in the absence of any real evidence that suggests such culpability exists.

However, both officials and lay observers have now been exposed to the uncontested nonsensical allegations of Berezovsky and his associates that started everything. Subsequent "confirmation bias" has led to the successive fabricated stories being accepted unquestioningly as being truthful.

Isn't it time to realize that this case has become contaminated, not by polonium, but by falsehoods? The chance of ever finding the truth under these conditions is exactly zero.

There are those who would argue against that.

First is Sir Robert Owen, the corner and Inquiry chair. Being past mandatory retirement age from the High Court, he'd be forced out to pasture. He'd also lose the opportunity for success on this high-profile case to top off and burnish his career.

Second are the Berezovsky associates. Their tenacity in pursuing their allegations suggests that they have some kind of payoff in mind.

And, third is David Cameron, the British prime minister. He reinstated the witch hunt for Russian culpability. Perhaps he believed it would make him look brave amidst the fervor to sanction and condemn Putin over the Ukrainian crisis.

It seems to me that these players have a vested interest in perpetuating the nonsense.

But, the only responsible reaction to this utter mess is to admit that the truth is unattainable. Further British national embarrassment would be avoided by admitting this.

Owning up to this reality would also have the potential for, in some way, relaxing dangerous international tensions.

Those handling the Litvinenko matter from the start have done a bad job. The case has been botched beyond rescue. Continuing to pretend that a reliable means exists for finding the truth will only perpetuate the morally corrupt process that has been endemic all along.

Clearly there is little chance of ever finding a truth that can be believed.

The honest course is to acknowledge that the truth is unattainable, and to just dismiss the case once and for all. That's the only reasonable solution.

Appendix I
Updates and Clarifications

AlexanderLitvinenko.Info is a website that has been set up to serve as an adjunct to this book. It will remain active for at least one year from the book's publication date.

If information emerges that is pertinent to the points made in *Litvinenko Murder Case Solved*, I'll post it there. The website is not intended to provide updates on developments in the news, however. Readers are encouraged to seek that information from active news organizations. Be mindful, however, of their propensities for distorting information as I've shown in this book. Apply the lessons you've learned here to news stories you subsequently see.

New postings will likely be erratic. Readers who want to keep up on whatever new is posted are encouraged to avail themselves of the various free services available for providing alerts. A search on the term "detect website updates" will get you a list of possible service providers.

The website is intended neither to be a blog, nor a forum for discussion. However, I am interested in receiving substantive feedback from readers. Identification of any factual errors will be warmly received, as will be the identification of any pertinent points that might I have missed. I'd prefer not to engage in debates over points of view, however.

You may contact me at WilliamDunkerley@AlexanderLitvinenko.Info.

Appendix II
About the Author

William Dunkerley is a media business analyst and consultant specializing in post-communist countries. He is a Senior Fellow at the American University in Moscow. Mr. Dunkerley has written extensively for the media management magazine *Sreda*, and has been published in major newspapers in the region.

A featured speaker at media business conferences in seven post-communist countries, including at the World Congresses of the International Federation of Journalists and the World Association of Newspapers, he has also appeared on national radio and TV in Eastern Europe and the former Soviet Union.

Mr. Dunkerley is also the author of *The Phony Litvinenko Murder* (www.omnicompress.com/plm), a book that debunks false media reports concerning the death of reputed spy Alexander Litvinenko; *Ukraine in the Crosshairs* (www.omnicompress.com/ukr), a common sense analysis of what's really behind the Ukrainian crisis; and *Medvedev's Media Affairs* (www.omnicompress.com/mma), focusing on Russia's media sector and its foibles.

He is principal of William Dunkerley Publishing Consultants, and editor and publisher of two industry publications: *Editors Only* (www.editorsonly.com) and the *STRAT Newsletter* (www.stratnewsletter.com).

Omnicom Press

Omnicom Press, publisher of this book, was founded in 1981 to offer publishing products and printing services. It now offers print-on-demand books and e-books. The e-books can be read on PCs, laptops, notebooks, tablets, e-readers, and smartphones. (www.omnicompress.com)